This book is a

Gift

from

_____

to

_____

on the occasion of

_____

date

_____

DOING THE IMPOSSIBLE

© Ayo Lawal
Ayo Lawal International
Lagos Nigeria
E-mail: ayolawal@ayolawal.com
Website: www.ayolawal.com

DOING THE IMPOSSIBLE
ISBN 978-978-931-905-3
Copyright 2015 by
GEM Enterprises, Lagos, Nigeria
Tel: +234 8161816869
E-mail: info@gementerprisesng.com

Published by GEM Enterprises
Lagos Nigeria

DOING THE IMPOSSIBLE

Walk In Absolute Dominion

AYO LAWAL

DEDICATION

To the physically challenged among us who daily aspire to do the impossible. May the visions of your heart swallow up your physical challenges in victory.

To all my faithful friends and brothers and sisters who supported me on this book. Your belief in me is unequalled. Thank you.

To all those who have done the impossible in our days, and especially to Bishop David Oyedepo, whose life, experiences, testimonies, and attitude have contributed more significantly than anything else to my ability to do the impossible.

Most especially for me, to the greatest One within you, the

power to do the impossible, and to all those who help to share it's testimony.

I dedicate this work.

Doing easily what
others find
difficult is talent,
doing what is
impossible
for talent is genius.

———   ———

HENRY FEDERIC AMIEL

Doing The Impossible — 10

ACKNOWLEDGMENT

In writing a book about this all-important subject—dominion, I want to acknowledge the great influence my mentor, Bishop David Oyedepo, the Chancellor, Covenant University, has had on my life and ministry. As long as I can remember you have always endeavoured to live a life of absolute dominion.

Your teachings on this dominion-conferring subject including your book, *Satan Get Lost!* and your own examples as you live your life without satan having a say has helped me learn in life to operate at a frequency of mystery where the enemy does not have a say... a strange sphere of existence where nothing is impossible.

Oh, yes! This sphere may be strange but it is also stupendous! And I thank God for it.

Today people can defy the enemy spit on him and even dethrone him simply by applying the incredible truths of God's word that I have had the privilege of sharing with them.

And now as I commit the same words into writing, I know that the same effect will be felt wherever these words are shared all around the world.

THE MANDATE

Go, preach excellence…raise the people fom the dust and bring them into glory.

Doing The Impossible — 14

CONTENTS

FOREWORD

I was at a meeting a few years ago where Pastor E. A. Adeboye, the General Overseer of The Redeemed Christian Church of God, was ministering on the topic, *Reversing the Irreversible*. The major question on my mind while he was speaking was, "How do you reverse what is irreversible?" By the end of the ministration, my question had been answered.

When Ayo handed a copy of his book to me, I realized that the book, *Doing the Impossible*, and Pastor Adeboye's message, *Reversing the Irreversible*, have the same underlying principles.

Doing the Impossible is a timely message from a fresh and truly unique perspective that challenges us to embrace the greatness that God has deposited in us. It causes us to recognize our true identity in God and build super strength to enforce it through stalwart study of God's word.

As you go through this one-of-kind, highly-inspiring and life-transforming book, you will not only realize but also testify that with God all things are possible!

KUNLE OYEGADE
Managing Director
Mopheth Nigeria Limited

PREFACE

> A consistent man believes in destiny,
> a capricious man in chance
> – BENJAMIN DISRAELI

For sin (satan) shall not have dominion over you, for ye are not under the law but under grace.
ROMANS 6:14 (Paraphrase Mine)

This is the plan of God for you.

God is sounding an alarm:

"Dominion is what you are created to have, therefore dominion you will have!"

Bishop Oyedepo taught, "You are not born again to suffer again." Friend, I can't agree more! That means – your new birth experience is God's strategic plan to exempt you from all forms of suffering. It is also heaven's strategy to expose you to all forms of enjoyment. It is our destiny to enjoy the abundance of all good things in their infinite varieties and innumerable aspects. So for you to be suffering where you are born to be shinning is aslap on your new birth.

You will not suffer.

This book has been masterfully designed to help you appreciate the spiritual mirror of your new kingdom status. So as you read, be a doer, and not a reader only. Readers only are like a man observing his natural face in a mirror; for he observes himself, goes away, and immediately forgets what kind of man he was. I know this is not the kind of person you want to be. Notable author, Johann Wolfgang Von Goethe once asserted", Knowing is not enough; we must apply. Wishing is not enough; we must do."

So don't just read. Do!

It is our time for dominion. But the hour for dominion must also be the hour for doers, or all the dominion we dream of walking in might end up as dreams, and never become a reality. So let's brace up and get determined to be not just readers, but also doers.

It is our turn for absolute dominion.

The doers are lining up already

You will not miss your place in it.

The alarm is sounding again:

"You shall have dominion over sin and satan, for you are under grace and not under law."

> A man who suffers before it is necessary
> suffers more than is necessary.
> SENECA

INTRODUCTION:

Why I Wrote This Book

Oh, yes! All things are possible. Supernatural health is possible. Superlative wealth is possible. Peaceful family life is possible. Academic excellence is possible. Business breakthrough is possible. Unprecedented church growth is possible. Friend, all things are possible. How? God said it and I believe it hook, line and sinker. In fact, I believed so thoroughly, I removed the word *impossible* from my "mental dictionary."

It is my absolute delight that you are reading this seasoned book today. I really thank God for your life because I believe this material is a setup by God to birth a new move that is going to herald a sporadic lift in your life. It will be such an exciting and adventuresome venture, and at the end of it all, you will finally know that all things are possible. For all things are yours.

It is our destiny to do the impossible. In the ninth chapter of the book of Mark, Jesus said, "If you can believe, all things are possible to him who believes". That you are holding this God-inspired, Spirit-indwelt and power-packed book reveals a lot. And the fact that you are reading reveals even more. It reveals your burning desire for a larger improvement in all areas of life – spiritual, physical, financial, material, etc. It is also a pointer to the fact that you believe in possibilities and would like to experience it in practical terms, and even help others to experience it too! Friend, it is our destiny to do the impossible and the impossible we will do.

Something is about to happen. It will be ear tingling! It will be mouth-gapping! It will be mind-blowing! It will be a major breakthrough. And it is going to happen in your favour. Please set yourself and get ready.

We are in the era of possibilities. As a student of revival, divine awakening and divine movement, I believe nothing is impossible. Absolutely nothing! I believe with God all things are possible. I also believe there are people with whom nothing is impossible. For example, our covenant patriarchs like Moses, Joshua, Gideon, Paul, waged a good warfare to turn all impossibilities into possibilities when all things seemed impossible.

Also, uncommon achievers like Albert Einstein, Leonardo de Vinci, Martin Luther King Jr., Nelson Mandela, Abraham Lincoln, Bill Gates who fought every inch of the way to convert every impossibility into possibilities when all things seemed impossible.

What I intend to do through this God-inspired, God-indwelt and eye-opening book is to take you by hand and walk you to the door that leads to the realm where this strange class of people operate, to deliver to you keys with which you can unlock the door to the realm of possibilities.

However, the responsibility to unlock the door and walk through it is yours. I hope you are ready to accept responsibility to approach this door, unlock it, and walk in the newness of life that this opportunity offers you. "The price of greatness is responsibility," says Winston Churchill, Former British prime minister.

It is our season of greatness. But the season of greatness must also be the season of responsibility. Remember the story of Mary the mother of Jesus when the angels came to break the news of the miracle baby to her? Luke told us:

> Then Mary said to the angel, "How can this be, since I do not know a man?" And the angel answered and said to her, "The Holy Spirit will come upon you, and the power of the Highest will overshadow you; therefore, also, that Holy One who is to be born will be called the Son of God. Now indeed, Elizabeth your relative has also conceived a son in her old age; and this is now the sixth month for her who was called barren. For with God nothing will be impossible." Then Mary said, "Behold the maidservant of the Lord! Let it be to me according to your word." And the angel departed from her (to go and carry out what Mary believed and said)
>
> LUKE 1:34-38 (Paraphrase Mine)

Mary did not say to the angel, "No, Lord, this is impossible." No. No. No. Rather, she literally said, "Yes, Lord, I believe this is possible." What an attitude!

There is no question without an answer There is no problem without a solution. Looking through the history of time, I have observed people like Mary, the mother of Jesus, who have handled seemingly insurmountable problems through simple alliance and compliance with principles and turned them around. Here, Mary attuned herself with the principle of faith. And her faith levelled her seemingly insurmountable mountain. Stephen Covey, a noted author and lecturer, defined principles as guidelines for human conduct that are proven to have enduring, permanent value.

Friend, principles and keys are synonymous terms. As you continue to flip through the pages of this book, I shall be placing in your hand necessary, vital and essential keys with which you can unlock the golden door to the greatest season of your life…your season of limitless possibilities! So brace up! Something is about to happen!

Small keys can unlock great doors of treasures.

Just one principle can terminate many years of affliction. The principles you will discover will skyrocket you to the sphere of life where there are no laws, limits or boundaries; a sphere of existence where even satan, your arch enemy does not have a say They are scriptural and powerful principles. They will change your life… instantly…forever! So please get ready!

And, please listen to this: Following the graphic example of Mary, the mother of Jesus, you cannot hear God's word without a human agent. In Romans 10:14, Paul asked, "How shall they hear without a preacher?"

You cannot believe the word of God that you have not heard. Paul added, "How shall they believe in him who they have heard? (Romans 10:14)

It is the word of God that you believe that helps you to do the impossible. Jesus affirmed, "If you can believe, all things are possible to him who believes." (Mark 9:23)

I strongly believe that I am one of the human agents that God has dispatched to my generation to deliver His message in this *mess-age*. I believe that those who embrace this message in faith will be elevated by it, and those who despise it in doubt will be damned by it. What I want to do is to show you the "key" log with which you can clear every log jam you may be experiencing today. So friend, the responsibility to chose which side you want to fall is yours. Your reality is sequel to your responsibility. So make your choice.

Statistics have proven that only 10 per cent of those who buy a book read past the first chapter. Perhaps this is the reason for the undoing of many that we see around us today. Don't be part of the statistics that do not read past the first chapter of a book.

This book has been designed to help you gain a unique insight into the prophetic plan of God for the saints and also locate your place in this prophetic agenda.

As an agent of God's word, I desperately want to help you.

I believe nothing is impossible.

I also believe YOU CAN DO THE IMPOSSIBLE.

So I wrote this book.

> If you aren't fired with enthusiasm, you will
> be fired with enthusiasm
> **VINCE LOMBARDI**
> American Football Coach

PART ONE

1

Travailing
As A Sheep

I am willing to put
myself through
anything;
temporary pain or
discomfort
means nothing to me
as long as I can see
that the experience will
take me to a
new level.

DIANA NYAD, Swimmer

1

THE SHEPHERD
AND THE SHEEP

*The Lord is my shepherd (and I am His sheep), I shall not
want. He makes me lie down in green pastures, he leads me
beside the still waters. He restores my soul, he leads me in the
paths of righteousness for his name's sake. Yea, though I walk
through the valley of the shadow of death (in my travail), I
will fear no evil (roaring lion); for You are with me; Your rod
and Your staff, they comfort me. You prepare a table before me
in the presence of my enemies, You anoint my head with oil
(power); my cup (of triumphant victory) runs over (as I
prevail). Surely goodness and mercy shall follow me all the
days of my life; And I will dwell in the house of the LORD
forever*

PSALMS 23:1-6 (Paraphrase Mine)

The sheep is sometimes used to symbolise Christian believers A careful understanding of a sheep's habits (of following, feeding, learning, growing, committing, refreshing, sacrificing, etc) reflects the quality character traits that are to be developed in Christian believers In fact, it was used to symbolise Christ in Isaiah's prophecy The prophet declared, "He was led as a lamb to the slaughter, and as a sheep before its shearer is silent, so He opened not his mouth" (Isaiah 53:7).

It was also used to symbolise the First Century Christians. In Romans 8:35-39, Paul declared:

> *As it is written: "For your sake we are killed all day long, we are counted as sheep for the slaughter" Who shall separate us from the love of Christ? shall tribulation, or distress, or persecution, or famine, or nakedness, or peril, or sword? As it is written, For thy sake we are killed all day long, we are counted as sheep for the slaughter Nay, in all these things we are more than conquerors through him that loved us. For I am persuaded that neither death, nor life, nor angels, nor principalities, nor powers, nor things present, nor things to come, Nor height, nor depth, nor any other creature, shall be able to separate us from the love of God, which is in Christ Jesus our Lord.*

In 1993, just a few months after I got saved, God began to visit me with visions and revelations. In one of these visions, there is this particular long-drawn out one where God revealed to me that I will end up in the ministry of the gospel.

I was sitting with some friends that I had before I met Christ. We were all in a place as our custom was, in our school uniforms - white short-sleeved shirts and navy blue shorts, saying dirty jokes…laughing at them. Suddenly a strange feeling came over me and I stood to my feet and I began to urinate on my body. I felt dirty. I felt embarrassed. But there and there were my friends, still doing their own thing without even noticing what had just happened to me.

Later, I saw myself lying flat on my face to the ground before a small gate of about three feet which led to a compound with a building as big as the eye could see. The compound also was as far as the eye could see. I lay down for a couple of minutes, in so much fear and trembling.

Then, a man walked up to me and said, "We have chosen you. Whatever you need, ask and it will be given to you." Then, he introduced me to another man who was seated somewhere around the building. Then I saw myself in an open field. It was so wide I could not see the end of it. As I stood there, I had a strong feeling that something was going to happen so I began to pray, "Lord, help me! Lord, help me!"

Then I looked and I saw a flock of sheep and a herd of cattle. Both kept in the same area but separated by a wooden ranch. I knew I needed to make a decision so I chose the flock of sheep. Spontaneously and momentarily, just as soon as I made my decision, a black hideous being jumped on me from a plain and we started wrestling. We wrestled and wrestled until I back slammed and pinned him to the ground. As soon as his back hit the ground, another black hideous being came out of the dark with a fork in his hand and rolled the wrestler away from me. I lifted my two hands and began to say "Thank you, Jesus! Thank you, Jesus!" I woke up and I realized that it had been a vision.

The life of a Christian believer is in two stages. I believe that was one of the message that God was trying to pass across to me through that vision. There is the *Sheep Stage* And there is the *Lion Stage*. The *sheep stage* is where we have to travail like a woman in labour to bring forth our destiny. So many golden destinies end up being aborted instead of being brought forth because of the lack of endurance during the time of labour. So many beautiful dreams end up at the cemetery because of their stubbornness and unwillingness to stand the test of travail.

Any woman that has ever laboured to bring forth a child will tell you that the time of labour is always a hard time. But they will also tell you that the joy that follows is worth the pain that comes with labour.

We have to be brought forth. We have to be born. But there must be travail first. The time of travail is the time to endure the pains – pains of prayer, fasting, dedication, diligence, discipline, and the likes. Something very interesting happened in Matthew 20:20-23 that I believe will help us to appreciate this principle. A family came to Jesus seeking His favour for enthronement. See what happened:

> *Then the mother of Zebedee's sons came to Him (Jesus) with her sons, kneeling down and asking something from him.*

And He (Jesus) said to her, "What do you wish?" She said to Him (Jesus), "Grant that these two sons of mine may sit, one on Your right hand and the other on the left, in Your kingdom. But Jesus answered and said, "You do not know what you ask. Are you able to drink the cup that I am about to drink, and be baptized with the baptism that I am baptized with?" They said to Him, "We are able." So He (Jesus) said to them, "You will indeed drink my cup, and be baptized with the baptism that I am baptized with; but to sit on my right and on my left is not mine to give, but it is for those for whom it is prepared by My Father."

"My cup" here connotes suffering. "The baptism" here means sacrifice. In other words, Jesus was telling Mrs. Zebedee and her two sons, James and John that they should not be too eager to enjoy enthronement in His kingdom because they will have to endure some suffering and make some sacrifices before they can enjoy enthronement. He wanted them to have a second thought as to whether they think the prize is worth the price in the first place. See how Luke 22:40-45 painted the cup and the baptism:

When He (Jesus) came to the place, He (Jesus) said to them, "Pray that you may not enter into temptation. And He (Jesus) was withdrawn from them about a stone's throw, and He (Jesus) knelt down and prayed, saying, "Father, if it is Your will, take this cup away from Me; nevertheless not My will, but Yours be done." Then an angel appeared to Him from heaven, strengthening him. And being in agony, He prayed more earnestly. Then His (Jesus) sweat became like great drops of blood falling down to the ground. When He (Jesus) rose up from prayer, and had come to His disciples, He found them sleeping from sorrow

What a suffering! What a sacrifice! This is what Jesus, the good Shepherd referred to as "My cup" and "the baptism". And of course, we all know the end of the story: Jesus bled, died, rose on the third day and now lives at the right hand of the Father God in majesty on high. But before receiving the accolades, he had to experience the agony.

This is what Jesus reiterated in Luke chapter 12:49-50:

I came to send fire on the earth, and how I wish it were already kindled! But I have a baptism to be baptized with, how distressed I am till it is accomplished!

We have to be brought forth. We have to be born. But there must be travail first. The travail may be hard but the harvest will justify the pain of our travail. Paul admonishes us, *"You therefore must endure hardness as a good soldier of Jesus Christ"* (2 Timothy 2:3).

Jim Rollins said there are two kinds of pain in life – the pain of discipline and the pain of regret. According to Rollins, the pain of discipline weighs ounces while the pain of regret weighs tons. The pain of discipline can be likened to the travail of man. Jesus endured the pain of discipline and ended up as the King of kings; Joseph endured the pain of discipline and ended up as the Prime Minister of Egypt. See how travail can be justified by triumph. But before triumph is travail. That's what the prophet Isaiah reiterated:

Before she travailed, she brought forth; before her pain came, she was delivered of a manchild. Who hath heard such a thing? Who hath seen such things? Shall the earth be made to bring forth in one day? Or shall a nation be born at once? for as soon as Zion travailed, she brought forth her children.

ISAIAH 66:7-8 (KJV)

Every triumph is traceable to travail. Show me a man that is travailing today and I will point to you a man that will triumph tomorrow. Martin Luther King Jr., of the United States, Mahatma Gandhi of India and Nelson Mandela in South Africa and other lesser known social deliverers around the world, laid down their lives and future to make civil rights available to disadvantaged individuals, communities and even nations. They travailed to birth their nations; they travailed to bring forth their rights as human beings. Today because of their tireless labour, we can all live without the fear of oppression, depression and harassment through slavery

Even Jesus, our Deliverer had to travail as a sheep before his lion destiny could be delivered. Isaiah recorded that *"...he is brought as a lamb to the slaughter, and as a sheep before her shearers..."* (Isaiah 53:7).

Our sheep nature can be likened to a pregnant woman, and the child in the womb, the lion nature. Only those who labour in the sheep nature will deliver the lion nature. Just as a pregnant woman must go into travail before her child is born, so also must one travail as a sheep before the lion can be born.

"We all like sheep…" These are the words of Isaiah the prophet emphasizing the sheep nature of man. In the life of every man that is born into this world, there is a sheep stage. No wonder, David called Jesus his Shepherd. Jesus referred to people as sheep having no shepherd. The sheep-Shepherd concept is not only an Old Testament thing; it is as real today as it was then. (Psalms 23:1; Matthew 9:36)

The Spirit Himself bears witness with our spirit that we are the children of God, and if children, then heirs— heirs of God and joint heirs with Christ, if indeed we suffer with him, that we may also be glorified together. For I consider that the sufferings of this present time are not worthy to be compared with the glory which shall be revealed in us. For the earnest expectation of the creation eagerly waits for the revealing of the sons of God. For the creation was subjected to futility, not willingly, but because of Him who subjected it in hope; because the creation itself also will be delivered from the bondage of corruption into the glorious liberty of the children of God. For we know that the whole creation groans and labors with birth pangs together until now.

ROMANS 8:16-22

The Lord is our Shepherd, not our hireling. We have played all manners of characters— bulls, wolves, cows, goats, dogs, serpents, cobras, foxes— all in the name of coverup. All these characters are for the hireling. What we have being doing all this while is hypocrisy and it does not lead anywhere! It is time we take on our covenant identity. Jesus said: "I AM THE GOOD SHEPHERD." Jesus could have referred to Himself as the good hireling but He did not. Rather, He spoke decidedly emphatically and convincingly. He said: I AM THE GOOD SHEPHERD.

We are in the last days. The last days are dangerous days. We must not engage our destiny by staying outside with the bulls, wolves, cows, goats, dogs, serpents, cobras and foxes. Like David, let's run to the good Shepherd and say "Lord, you are our Shepherd."

> *But outside are dogs and sorcerers and sexually immoral and murderers and idolaters, and whoever loves and practices a lie.*
> REVELATION 22:15

Who are dogs? Those who were once inside heaven's kingdom, but are now outside, in hell's kingdom because they lack of endurance; and those who return to "old things" that ought to have passed away. They belong to the same fold as the bulls, wolves, cows, goats, serpents, cobras and foxes.

2 Peter 2:22 reiterated this:

> *But it is happened to them according to the true proverb, "A dog is returned to his own vomit," and, "a sow having washed to her wallowing in the mire."*

Dogs are those who return to their vomit. A while ago, I met a lady who used to attend the same church I did (not

The Elevation Church). Then I asked her if she still worships in that church, as I had not seen her in quite a while. "Oh, no!" she replied. "I am back to being a muslim. In fact, I am married now, and my husband is a muslim."

This was really sad.

Today you may find yourself travailing in the sheep stage. But don't worry, and don't go back to your vomit. Always remember your triumph is just around the corner. Why? You are a lion in sheep clothing.

> When you dare to dream, dare to follow that dream; dare to suffer through the pain, sacrifice, self-doubts and friction from the world.
> LAURA SCHLESINGER, Talk-show host

2

A LION IN
SHEEP OLHING

> We al as lion…
> – AYO LAWAL

Once upon a time, a lioness was pregnant with a lion cub. Then, the cub finally arrived. Then later, when it was time for the lion cub to learn to hunt, the lioness took the cub out on an adventure somewhere around the jungle. Unfortunately something went wrong and the lioness could not locate the cub. A farmer found the baby lion in his farm and brought him home to keep. He kept the cub with his flock. Then they would go for watering and a lion would come to attack them. All the sheep would run back to the farm to hide from the lion, and the lion cub would join them. They would go grazing and a lion would show up and all the sheep would head for the farm to hide, along with the cub. Thus, the lion cub continued to live like a sheep, drinking water, eating grass, and bleating around the farmland. It was very pathetic!

Well, it was not over. One afternoon, while they were drinking water, a lion showed up to attack them. As usual, all the sheep ran back to the farm to hide from the lion. The lion cub looked into the water, saw his face, looked at the lion and said, "I look like the lion. I don't look like the sheep running." So when the lion got closer to him, the lion cub just wagged his tail and went to join him. From that day the lion cub ceased to live like a sheep and started to live as a lion.

Life is in phases. Paul said: "when I was a child I thought as a child but when I became an adult, I put away childish things." The lion often symbolizes human beings. Jacob referring to Judah said, " Judah is a lion's whelp; from the prey, my son, you have gone up. He bows down, he lies down as a lion; and as a lion, who shall rouse him?" (Genesis 49:8-12)

Habit determines habitat. Where you find yourself today may be as result of your habits of yesterday. If you want to change where you are, you may need to change your habit first. Habit dictates habitat. Old habits are breakable. New habits are formable. A careful understanding of a lion's habits (of learning, growing, hunting, committing, refreshing, roaring, etc) will help us identify the quality character traits that we must develop to evolve from the sheep-phase into the lion-phase of our lives. John Milton said, "As the morning shows the day so the boy shows the man." We belong to God's Lion family. Remember the prophet Isaiah refers to Jesus as The Lion of the tribe of Judah.

In Micah 5:8, the Bible says:

> *And the remnant of Jacob shall be among the Gentiles in the midst of many peoples like a lion among the beasts of the forest, like a young lion among the flocks of sheep, who, if he passes through, both treads down and tears in pieces, and none can deliver.*

Every one born into the family of God is therefore born into the Lion Family; a cosmic family with countless possibilities. However, our heritage of countless possibilities may remain only a dream until we understand our identity in this cosmic family. Why? Our identity becomes our backbone during the days when everything looks practically impossible.

Friend, we are in the "jungle" era of the church. And the lion is the king of the jungle. So for you to still beliving as a sheep in the "jungle" age will be a slap on your redemption. So wake up! Wake up the sleeping lion within you!

A while ago, one of the banks in Nigeria, where I worked at the time, sent me on training. During the training, the facilitator asked the participants to mention their favourite pet and state reasons why they had made their choice. Our facilitator said this activity would help each participant understand their personality by identifying their most desired pet. Some people mentioned monkeys, cats, and the likes. When it got to my turn, I told her my preferred pet was a lion because its bold, adventurous and fearless. Immediately I mentioned my preferred pet, the entire class went into a tumult because the other participants could not understand why of all animals in the world, I would choose a lion as a pet.

My little children of whom I travail in birth again until Christ be formed in you.
                                                    GALATIANS 4:19 (KJV)

Lambs are slain. Lions prevail. Remember satan is not a lion. He is not like a lion. He only acts like a lion. If you refuse to assume your lion status, the devil will roar like a lion, prey on you, and eventually slaughter you like a lamb.

Some years ago, Bishop Oyedepo got home one night after a meeting and his wife told him she had a miscarriage. Without hesitation, Bishop Oyedepo reacted and said, "It cannot happen! Can I have my food please?" And that was the end of miscarriage. The pregnancy that was to be preyed upon by the blood-thirsty devils pastors one of the most vibrant churches in the United Kingdom today. Why? The one that was born a lion chose to roar when the counterfeit lion showed up. You are born to prevail, not to be preyed upon. So sit up and take charge!

Our identity is unfolded in two facets first, we are going to travail as sheep. Then, we are going to prevail as lions. This was the case with Jesus greatest man who ever lived. In Revelation chapter 5, He was referred to as the Lion of the tribe of Judah, and was also referred to as the Lamb in the same chapter Of course, it was the Jesus-lion that prevailed (not the Jesus-lamb) Friend, we are born lions, we can't afford to die losers. Like the lion cub that lost its way we have belittled ourselves for too long. It is time we beginto "be-lion" ourselves.

Jesusfirst cameasa sheep.Revelation5: the apostlesaid, *"And I looked, and behold,the midst ofhte throne...and the midsbftheelders,stoodLambasthought hadbeenslain."*

In Isaiah53:7,the prophetcried, *"He wasledasalambtothe slaughter,andasasheepbeforeitssharers..."*

> *"He wasledasalambtotheslaughter"A Lambasthought hadbeenslain."*

Whatasuffering?Oh, to bedelivered!

But it didn't endthere.Later, hegrewinto alion. Andthisis theplanof Godfor allHis children. Youareborn asasheep. Then latergrowup to bealion. This iswhatJohntold usin Revelation5:4-5:

> *Sol weptmuchbecausenomanwasfoundworthy.....one oftheeldersaidtome,"Do notweep...thelionofthetribeof JudahTheRoobfDavid,hasprevailed...*

Though Jesus was destined to do the impossible as a lion, He had to travail asa sheepfirst. And asjoint heirswith him, He hassentus to goanddo the same.That iswhatwe hearin Romans8:16-17:

We arethe children of God: And if children, then heirs; heirsof God, andjoint-heirs with Christ; if sobethatwe sufferwith him, thatwemaybealsoglorified together

We have suffered enough as sheep. Now it is our turn to shine as lions. Otherwise, our Christianity will be reduced to mere ashes. But that won't be your portion. Even Jesus, the Lion King did not promise us that.

The next time you hear anything roaring like a lion around you perhaps it has mistaken you for a sheep just roar back and the counterfeit lion will flee from you. Like some houseowners do in my part of the world, you may even write a signboard with this inscription: "Beware of dogs." I think the right inscription should be: "Beware of lions!"

> Man is what he believes.
> ANTHON CHEKHO

3

AWAKEN THE
LION WITHIN

> The person who cannot see the ultimate
> becomes a slave to the immediate.
> DR MYLES MUNROE

Understanding determines what happens. The redemptive work of Jesus offers us newness of life. So we cannot continue to bleat with the sheep after we have been redeemed as lions. We can't continue to eat grass with the sheep and expect to do the impossible. For us to continue scratching with the sheep is an insult on our redemption. Friend, wake up!

It is important for us to know that there are human sheep, human lions, human goats, human scorpion, human wolves and the likes. But we belong to the class of God by the virtue of our new birth.

As dear children of God, we now carry the DNA for believing the unbelievable and doing the impossible. As joint heirs with Christ, we now have authority to walk in absolute dominion. When we gave our lives to Christ we had a change of status that conferred absolute majesty on us. Our new lineage is a lion lineage. In Genesis chapter forty nine, Jacob our covenant patriarch blessing Judah referred to him as a lion:

> *Judah you are he whom your brothers shall praise, thy hand shall be on the neck of your enemies, your father's children shall bow down before you, Judah is a lion's whelp, from the prey my son you have gone up. He bow down, he lies down as a lion. And as a lion, who shall rouse him?*
>
> GENESIS 49: 8-9

This is what obtains in our family tree. Our new covenant lineage is a lion lineage. The premise of this jackpot section is to help us understand which of these categories we fall into, and also walk majestically in the light of it. We have passed from the sheep to the lion class. As beloved children of God, you and I now carry the lion DNA of Jesus. We are lions after the order of Jesus the Lion of the Tribe of Judah. We are born of strength, power, glory, honour, riches and majesty!

In fact, then and after the story I shared in chapter two, some of my classmates started calling me *Ayo Lion* just because I picked the lion as my most desired pet. I didn't reject the nickname because I understood better. We all need an understanding of our change of status after new birth. Then after we have understood it, we must go ahead to unleash it. Friend, we are just on the verge of an unusual unleashing of our supernatural status. Lions after the order of the Lion of the tribe of Judah are just about to be awakened. Beware!

Stop bleating. Its time you grow up. So grow up! If you don't grow up today, you may end up groaning tomorrow. So grow up. And please when you do, roar.

An Army of Lions

I remember a man of God praying for me back then in 1995. While praying he said prophetically "You will be a builder in My house." This prophecy amongst other things helped me appreciate that God is a Builder, and He has not retired from the building business He started before time and season in the book of Genesis. Even today He is constantly in His building business.

In Genesis He built the heavens and the earth, the animal kingdom, the plant kingdom, and created the sun, moon and the stars. Finally, God built man, and then, God rested. But I want to believe that God didn't rest to retire permanently from His building business. Oh, no! God is still very much into the building business. In fact, He told me in 2002 to build Him men and women who will be excellent in the society.

Come on, God is building a people.

A people of strength.

A people of affluence.

An army of power.

But it is also an army of lions.

There has never been an army (of lions) like the kind God is building at this time! See how Joel painted it:

> …a people come great and strong, the like of whom has never been, Nor will there ever be any such after them, even for many successive generations. A fire devours before them and behind them a flame burns; the land is like the Garden of Eden before them, and behind them a desolate wilderness; surely nothing shall escape them. There appearance is like the appearance of horses and like swift steeds so they run. With a noise like chariots over mountain tops they leap, like the noise of a flaming fire that devours the stubble, like a strong people set in battle array
>
> JOEL 2:2-5

What a great people!

What an army to be envied!

What an army of lions!

Heaven is sounding the trumpet louder yet:

"You are no more a sheep. You are now a lion. So brace up! Don't bury your destiny"

> An army of sheep led by a lion will always defeat an army of lions led by a sheep
> OLD PROVERB

4

THE HORROR
OF SIN

> Character is power.
> BOOKER WASHINGTON

Holiness is the pathway to God's power. Purity is a power booster anytime, any day, anywhere! Remember what God says in Genesis 1:28:

Then God blessed them and God said to them, "Be fruitful and multiply; fill the earth and subdue it; have dominion..."

Subdue means conquer, and it takes power to conquer. Power is a fundamental factor for establishing man's dominion on earth. The enormity of power demonstrated by the first man, Adam was so much that no other creature could question his authority. Not even the serpent, satan. But holiness was Adam's backbone; it was his purity that guaranteed his power.

satan is synonymous with sin. God is synonymous with

greatness. Sin is a power inhibitor. Purity is a power catalyst. We were born into greatness, not mediocrity. Man was created with dignity and power. But, the moment sin set in, man began to sink. One born of power suddenly descended to the level of a weakling. Satan stripped him of his greatness. It was a tragedy. This is the horror of sin!

God created the garden of Eden, a symbol of the primary design of the quality kind of life that God wanted for Adam. Then God put him in the garden to dress and keep it. But Adam lost it to the sin of disobedience. So he became a servant where he was once a king, just because sin found a doorway into his life. Eden was a showcase of the quality kind of life God originally intended for him. But he lost Eden to evil.

Samson was the gateway to divine supernatural power, but he lost it all on the thighs of Delilah. Sin destroyed Samson's destiny; Do not let it destroy yours. Stop dipping your hand into money that does not belong to you. Think and change. Sin is a trap from hell designed to ruin your life. Stop committing that sin before it stops you!

God is blowing His trumpet:

"HOLINESS! HOLINESS! HOLINESS UNTO GOD!"

Bishop David Oyedepo related this story:

A young man, an usher, was stealing from the offering basket, and he had done it so often, it had become his regular source of income. Then he was struck with tuberculosis. When he came and confessed to me, I told him to ask God for mercy. I also pleaded for mercy on his behalf. I desired for him to live, but he died.

Somebody else died, and on his deathbed, he confessed to impropriety of one million naira which he claimed to have returned.

Nothing can be more horrible than this.

He also related this one too:

In 1992, something happened in a certain church in one of our cities. Some fellows in the church rose against their pastor. One man particularly was the ringleader. He was raging and ranting, pointing accusing finger at the pastor. The pastor said, "let's be careful so that what happened to Ananias and Saphira will not happen here." The man stood up and began to talk. Right there and then, he slumped and died in the church there. His wife was there, she saw all that happened, so no one could say somebody killed him. He died in rebellion.

It is really horrible. That will never be your portion, in Jesus name!

> *The thief does not come except to steal, and to kill, and to destroy. I have come that they may have life, and that they may have it more abundantly.*
>
> JOHN 10:10

There is nothing more sorrowful than sin. There is nothing more colourful than character. Do not give the devil a place in your life, family or business. You have a destiny of excellence do not sell yourself short. The fact that everybody is doing it does not make it right, sir! You are a saint, not a sinner. So, recover yourself. And do it quickly because there is death in the pot!

> Change might not be fast and it isn't always easy. But with time and effort, almost any habit can be reshaped.
> CHARLES DUHIGG

Someone may say "I've really tried to stop smoking, but just can't help it. I guess it is my nature." Someone else may say "Well, apart from my wife, I don't sleep with other women, except my girlfriend."

It is not your nature to sin. Sin is a satanic nature. Holiness is your true intrinsic nature. It is your birthright. It is available. And, of course, it is attainable. It is over to you. It is over to you!

This is what 1 John 5:18 tells us:

We know that whoever is born of God does not sin; but he who has been born of God keeps himself, and that wicked one does not touch.

So you see you are not a womanizer or a drug addict because it is in your nature to do these things. You do them because you have not encountered the Spirit of holiness. What the Spirit of holiness does is to empower you supernaturally to live above sin and satan. The psalmist gives us a very striking insight into this truth:

Gird Your sword upon Your thigh, O Mighty One, with Your glory and Your majesty And in Your majesty ride prosperously because of truth, humility and righteousness; and Your right hand shall teach You awesome things. Your arrows are sharp in the heart of the king's enemies; the people fall under You. Your throne, O God, is forever and ever; a scepter of righteousness is the scepter of Your kingdom. You love righteousness and hate wickedness; therefore God, Your God, has anointed You with the oil of gladness above Your companions.

PSALM 45:3-7

So, the Spirit of holiness was the force behind all feats that happened in the life and ministry of Jesus. The Holy Ghost heavily anointed the King of kings; but holiness was His watchword. Holiness is the pathway to God's glory. Purity is the booster of power. Friend, it is time you chose the camp in which you want to belong.

For the devil to oppress you in your dream is a disgrace to your salvation. Earlier on, I mentioned that shortly after I gave my life to Christ, some demons would oppress me in my dream. I contacted the Spirit of holiness, and afterwards, instead of them oppressing me, I became the one chasing them about in my dreams. That is the efficacy of the power of the Spirit of holiness.

> The beginning of a habit is like an invisible thread, but every time we repeat the act we strengthen the strand, add to it another filament until it becomes a great cable and binds us irrevocably thought and act
> ORISON SWETT MARDEN

5

THE ISUE OF
IGNORANCE

> Thee is no mountain aywhere; every
> man's ignoance is his mountain.
> BISHOP AVID OOYEDEPO

As we move through history, the horrifying stench of ignorance continues to spread. The echoes of the cry for knowledge are heard throughout the halls of history, as individuals, communities, nations and generations seek to be free from the clutches of ignorance.

Ignorance is deadly I hate it. Ignorance is a killer disease. We must fight it. The Spirit is saying:

My people are destroyed for lack of knowledge.

HOSEA 4:6

This verse does not say they are destroyed for lack of prayer Neither does it say they are destroyed for lack of fasting. No. No. No. It says they are destroyed for lack of knowledge.

I remember when I was just growing up as a Christian. Then, God began to reveal to me that I was going to be a preacher. But, of course, I would not want bring shame to God. I would not want to disappoint my generation. So, I began to invest my money in books, tapes and other materials that I knew could help me in my personal development.

Friend, ignorance is an enemy it is not a friend. Let us fight it. Let me digress momentarily with the story of the woman with the issue of blood.

> *And, behold, a woman which was diseased with an issue of blood twelve years, came behind him (Jesus), and touched the hem of his garment. For she said within herself, If I may but touch his garment, I shall be whole. But Jesus turned him about, and when he saw her, He said, Daughter be of good comfort, thy faith hath made thee whole. And the woman was made whole from that hour.*
>
> MATTHEW 9:20-22 (KJV)

This woman had been afflicted by the devil for twelve years. But, thank God, she met Jesus, the word of God, and her affliction of many years ended in a single day.

Even today as we walk into the shallow shores of the ocean of the twenty-first century and take on the responsibility of the custodians of the new millennium, I believe we need a touch of Jesus, not to be healed of an issue of blood, but to be healed of an issue of ignorance.

They do not know, nor do they understand; they walk about in darkness; all the foundations of the world are unstable. I said, "You are gods, and all of you are children of the Most High. But you shall die like men, and fall like one of the princes."

PSALM 82:5-7

Why will they die like men? Why will they fall like one of the princes? They do not know! Why don't they know? The enemy corrupted their minds. See how Paul put it:

Whose minds the god of this age has blinded, who do not believe, lest the light of the gospel of the glory of Christ, who is the image of God, should shine on them.

2 CORINTHIANS 4:4

And because the enemy has corrupted their minds, they live like servants where they are destined to be kings. They live like parasites whereas they were born to be contributors. Remember the story of the lion cub? Although the baby lion was born to shine, it suffered because of the ignorance of its identity. We need to change our level and move from the corrupted level to the regenerate level. We must be 'spirited' by the Spirit of knowledge.

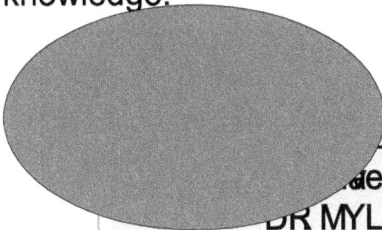

...cannot see the ultimate
...e to the immediate.

DR MYLES MUNROE

6

SATAN ON
THE RUN

To sit back and let fate play its hand out
and never influence it is not the way
man was meant to operate.
JOHN GLENN, Astronaut

*See then that you walk circumspectly, not as fools but as wise,
redeeming the time, because the days are evil.*
EPHESIANS 5:15-16

Satan is the greatest enemy of man. And, of course,
he knows that he needs to get all the time he can to
unleash his sheer cruelty on man. Revelations
12:12 echoes this:

*…Woe to the inhabitants of the earth…for the devil is come
down to you, having great wrath, because he knows that he
has but a short time*

God also recognizes the fact that satan, the archenemy of
man is time-sensitive, and God charges us to redeem our
time in order to retain and sustain our kingdom-status.

Then, we will be unbeatable- too strong to be challenged by the enemy

Victory takes time. When they were to kill all the wise men in Babylon, Daniel, a young man who had an understanding of time said unto the King, "Give us time," and it was not long before Daniel stumbled on the solution to the King's problem. Time is a basic prerequisite for triumph. (DANIEL 2:16-17)

God has entrusted each of us with the same time – twenty-four hours a day. We are allotted but a fleeting moment in time on the scale of eternity. And the earth's clock is ticking away very fast. It is high time we begin to accept responsibility for our destiny. It is high time we make the most of our life. It is high time we wake up in the middle of the night, roll up our sleeves, burn our tongues drinking hot tea, flip our Bibles open, kneel down, and tell the devil: "Time up, satan!" Friend, it is time to sit up.

> *Do not look upon me, because I am dark, because the sun has tanned me. My mother's sons were angry with me, they made me the keeper of the vineyards, but my own vineyard I have not kept.*
>
> SONGS OF SOLOMON 1:2

Avoid being a busybody in other men's matters. "*Study to do your business,*" says Apostle Paul.

Read this too:

> *Now as the king passed by, he cried out to the king and said,*

"Your servant went out into the midst of the battle and there, a man came over and brought a man to me, and said, 'Guard this man; if by any means he is missing, your life shall be for his life, or else you shall pay a talent of silver.' While your servant was busy here and there, he was gone. Then the king of Israel said to him, "So shall your judgment be; you yourself have decided it."

1 KINGS 20:39-40

You will not suffer.

From the passage in Songs of Solomon, the writer did not suffer because he was black; he suffered because he was a busybody in other men's matter. He suffered because he did not know how to redeem his time. If you are a busybody, you will suffer what sinners suffer. So repent.

But let none of you suffer as a murderer, a thief, an evildoer, or as a busybody in other people's matters.

1 PETER 4:15

You are not born again to suffer again. You are a saint, not a sinner. So, recover yourself. Time is running out.

In asmuch as I want you to be time-sensitive, I will also like you to know that it doesnot matter how big your dream is, God is not running away. A lot of people are in prisons all over the world, because they want quick money. Be time-sensitive. Attune yourself to the principle of management as ordained by God; and when you do, please be effective.

If you think this book is going to offer you a quick fix on how to be successful or victorious, then you are making the biggest mistake. There are no short cuts to success. This book offers you scriptural yet practical principles that will change your paradigm, and then put you in a covenant place in God. These principles will change your life dramatically…forever. So brace up and get ready for it!

It is your time to do the impossible, and the impossible you will do!

> Loss time is never found again
> BEN FRANKLIN

PART TWO

2

Understanding Your Lion Nature

Man is not the sum of
what he has but
the totality of what he
does not yet have,
of what he might have.

JEAN PAUL SARTRE

7

THE POWER OF INFORMATION

> "At home we have always regarded the dining table as the prime seat of learning. We planned it so it was impossible to see or hear a TV from the table, and it has paid dividends in the volume of ideas that have been shared over the evening meal."
> NOEL WHITAKER, Financial Advisor

E very victory in life is traceable to information. Information is the father of manifestation. Information is everything, like a notable author wrote.

I fell in love with the story of James Owen the first time I heard it. While still in high school, Owen desired to be a sport star, so he asked his coach what it would take to be a sport star. His coach told him about the four key factors to stardom: Determination, Dedication, Discipline and Attitude. James took advantage of that information, accepted the challenge, and went on to win four record-breaking gold medals at the 1926 Berlin Olympics. He set a record that remained unbreakable for more than two decades. This is an anecdote of doing the impossible, all on the platform of applied information. The coach must have told him about the four key factors to success in the presence of Owen's teammates, they probably heard it but did not apply it. Friend, correctly applied information is everything. Let's go get it.

The essence of what you are reading is to effect change – positive and profitable change. Based on our context there, information involves the collection of scriptural facts. A scriptural fact means revelation, which is the platform for a revolutionary Christian life. Revelation is a major prerequisite for revolution. After Gideon had been armed with the information that he received from the angel of the Lord, he just went with his men and disarmed the Midianites. It was a revolution! We are in the information age. To live outside information at this most crucial time is to end in deformation.

Prophetically, the church is programmed to trade information – vital kingdom information – at this most significant time. And as the church begins to do this, there shall be an unusual release of power from heaven above. And the dominion of the church will be unquestionable and unstoppable. The last day body will constitute the ruling power on earth. How? By trading scriptural information.

See what Daniel 11:32 says:

> Those who do wickedly against the covenant he shall corrupt with flattery, but the people who know their God shall be strong and carry out great exploits.

This is buttressed in chapter 24 of the book of proverbs:

> *A wise man is strong; yes, a man of knowledge increases strength.*
>
> PROVERBS 24:5

John G. Lake did the impossible. He was in South Africa when a plague broke out and thousands of people were dying. He challenged the doctors to take some of the foam from the mouths of the victims of the plague and examine it to be sure the germs were still alive. Then he told them to put the foam on his hand after which he was examined under a microscope. To the utter amazement of the doctors, all the germs were found dead.

Come on, friend, information is powerful; Information infuses strength, it makes you unbeatable- too strong to be defeated by the enemy!

God is building a people; a people of super strength; an army of exploit; and men and women that will excel in strength like the angels. How? They will also excel in knowledge like the angels. Remember how Elisha outran the chariot of Ahab? "but the people who know their God shall be strong, and carry out great exploits."

People exploding with signs wonders simply by trading scriptural information. They will excel in strength like the angels. The world will see them and say "The gods have come down in the likeness of men." All by the virtue of information that will be availableto the church from above.You will not missyour place.

> To the dul mind al natue is laden. To the illumined mind the whole world burns and sparkles with light
> WALDOS EMERSON

8

THE LION KING

Your greatness is measured
by your horizons."
MICHELANGEL

In Revelation 5:5-6, the John said:

> *But one of the elders said to me, Do not weep. Behold the
> lion of the tribe of Judah, the Root of David, has prevailed to
> open the scroll, and to loose its seven seals. And I looked, and
> behold, in the midst of the throne and of the four living
> creature, and in the midst of the elders, stood a Lamb as
> though it had been slain, having seven horns and seven eyes,
> which are the seven Spirits of God sent out into all the earth.*

I will never forget the Walt Disney animation film,
The Lion King. I have seen it over and over again
because I have found it to be inspiring. It tells the
story of a baby prince who became guilt-ridden, fled into
exile, lost his identity as the future King after being tricked
by his uncle into thinking he had killed his father.

The baby prince, Simba was born to Sarabi and Mufasa, the lion-rulers reigning over the Pride Lands. The cub was presented to their subjects, an enormous hoard of serengeti animals, by the wise mandrill Rafiki. However, Mufasa's envious younger brother, Scar, threatened by the birth of his nephew Simba, as he has been stripped of his status as heir presumptive to the throne through the prince's birth, conspires against Mufasa and Simba in secret in hopes of one day ruling over the Pride Lands.

Before long, Simba ages into an eager, bold, strong and adventurous little cub anxious at the prospect of one day taking over the throne. In an attempt to prove his strength and courage, Simba invites his closest friend Nala to venture out into the Elephant Graveyard (beyond the Pride Lands) with him, in spite of his father's cautions of the hazards of the area. After distracting their babysitter, Zazu the hornbill, the cubs escape to the graveyard but run into three starving hyenas called Shenzi, Banzai, and Ed with the intentions of hunting them. Nala and Simba try to flee from the clutches of the hyenas, though fortunately Mufasa arrives to his son's aid before long and wards them off. Afterward, Simba apologizes to the forgiving king, who explains the guardianship of the spirits of previous kings to him in the stars above.

Later, it is revealed that the hyenas were actually working under Scar's employment in exchange for food, and they are chastised for their failure in carrying out their master's evil plot. However, soon Scar receives inspiration for a deadly new plot and explains it to his followers. The following morning, Scar lures Simba to a canyon and triggers a stampede of wild beasts, tricking Mufasa into entering the same canyon in order to rescue his son. Fortunately King Mufasa manages to lead Simba to safety but is sent tumbling to his demise by Scar and is trampled to death by the wild beasts. A mournful Simba is convinced by his uncle that he is responsible for Mufasa's death and is exiled from the Pride Lands, and soon he meets a meerkat named Timon and warthog named Pumbaa. In song, they introduce a guilty Simba to their carefree lifestyle and, oblivious to the cub's royal heritage, invite Simba to come live with them in a gorgeous rainforest environment.

Eventually Simba develops into a fully-grown male lion who is still haunted by his past. While battling a hungry lioness after her attempts at hunting Pumbaa, he recognizes her as Nala and they meet again with a joyful reunion, much to Timon and Pumbaa's chagrin, feeling that a romance is blossoming between the pair. During the romantic evening, Nala pleads with Simba to return to the Pride Lands, which have been devastated in turmoil by Scar's tyrannical rule, but he refuses, still believing Scar's story, and the two split apart in fury. Under Rafiki's guidance of how to handle his grief, Simba receives a ghostly apparition in the sky from Mufasa's spirit urging him to return home, a message he takes to heart and leaves to brawl with Scar

With the assistance of Nala, Pumbaa, Timon, Sarabi, Rafiki, and the lionesses of Pride Rock, Simba engages in bloodthirsty combat with Scar and his rebels on a stormy night, Pride Rock goes up in flames due to lightning strike nearby At one point, Scar reveals to Simba that he was responsible for Mufasa's murder in actuality a truth that Simba manages to prod Scar into revealing to the residents of Pride Rock. Luckily Scar is defeated and attacked by his own betrayed hyenas, and Simba takes over the throne of Pride Rock. Months later, he fathers a cub after mating with Nala which Rafiki presents to the animals of the Pride Lands.

Interesting, isn't it? Unfortunately this is like the story of some of us. The devil tells us lies about the finished redemptive work by Jesus in order to hinder us from enjoying our covenant redemptive package He wants to stop us from walking in the reality of the life Jesus the King of kings and Lord of Lords has purchased for us. But we must suffocate the enemy before he stops us.

> *And they sang a new song saying: "You are worthy to take the scroll, and to open its seals, for You were slain, and have redeemed us to God by Your blood out of every tribe and tongue and people and nation, And have made us kings and priests to our God; and we shall reign on the earth."*
> REVELATION 5:9-10

Though like Simba, we are heirs to the throne, our ascension to the throne will not be a sudden act. It will be a process. There are vital covenant steps on our way to the throne. First of all, we need to…

9

BE BORN

I might have been born in a hovel, but I am determined to travel with the wind and the stars.
JACQUELINE COCHRAN, aviator

In Luke 2:8-12, the Bible records:

> *Now there were in the same country shepherds living out in the fields, keeping watch over their flock by night. And behold, an angel of the Lord stood before them, and the glory of the Lord shone around them, and they were greatly afraid. Then the angel said to them, "Do not be afraid, for behold, I bring you good tidings of great joy which will be to all people. For there is born to you this day in the city of David a Savior, who is Christ the Lord..."*

This is good news!

On the day of your birth, someone broke good news like this. This was good, and it gave you a place on earth, but there is a better type of news can be broken about us. This news is always broken in heaven about the rebirth of sinners. If we are to be engrafted into the company of people that do the impossible, the news of our birth has to be broken twice. One is done on earth, the second is done in heaven; The first is physical, the second is spiritual; Men rejoice more at one. The angels rejoice more at the other. Jesus said, *"There is joy in presence of the angels of God over one sinner who repent."* (Luke 15:10)

No wonder, Jesus told his disciples not to rejoice because they are born to do signs and wonders on earth, but to rejoice because they are reborn, and their heavenly birth certificate has been issued, sealed, stamped and delivered!

> *Then the seventy returned with joy, saying, "Lord, even the demons are subject to us in Your name." And He said to them, "I saw satan fall like lightning from heaven. Behold, I give you the authority to trample on serpents and scorpions and over all the power of the enemy, and nothing shall by any means hurt you. Nevertheless do not rejoice in this, that the spirits are subject to you, but rather rejoice because your names are written in heaven."*
>
> LUKE 10:17-20

In other words, Jesus wants us to rejoice most especially because we are born again. It is good thing to be born. But it is better to be born again. The premise of this chapter is to unveil the strategy of the new birth over mediocrity; and to uncover the mystery of new creation in guaranteeing our true and lasting freedom from all the embarrassment, harassment and reproach of our adversary, the devil. In John 1:1-14, concerning Jesus, the Lion of the Tribe of Judah (as we have already established from scriptural stand points), the message translation of the Bible says:

The Word was first, the Word present to God, God present to the Word. The Word was God, in readiness for God from day one.

Everything was created through him; nothing – not one thing! – came into being without him. What came into existence was Life, and the Life was light to live by. The Life-Light blazed out of darkness, the darkness couldn't put it out. There once was a man, his name John, sent by God to point out the way to the Life-Light. He came to show everyone where to look, who to believe in. John was not himself the Light; he was there to show the way to the Light. The Light-Life was the real thing: Every person entering life, he brings into light. He was in the world, the world was there through him, and yet the world didn't even notice. He came to his own people, but they didn't want him. But whoever did want him, who believed he was who he claimed and would do what he said, he made to be their true selves, their child-of-God selves. These are the God-begotten, not blood-begotten, not sex-begotten. The Word became flesh and blood, and moved into the neighbourhood. We saw the glory with our own eyes, the one-of-a-kind glory, like father, like son, generous inside and out, true from start to finish.

Lions are born. Like in the story of the lion cub, the lion

cub had to be born first before he could grow up to become a lion. This is the principle of procreation, and according to this principle, like begets like. A cow procreates a cow. A sheep procreates a sheep. So also a lion procreates a lion. And of course, the same principle applies to us today. So be born. Be born. Be born. And I mean, be born again!

There is a proverb from my birth home in Africa that says after a child has been born by his parent, the child has to rebirth himself if he is to make anything good of his life. And I cannot agree more! Why? I strongly believe that the proverb has its root in the Bible. The Bible teaches us to be reborn…regenerated completely–inside and out.

Many years back, after seeing Jesus do the impossible at different occasions, Nicodemus, a ruler of the Jews, came to Jesus by night and said, "Rabbi, we know that You are a teacher come from God; for no one can do these signs that You do unless God is with him." Jesus told him, "most assuredly, I say to you, unless one be born again, he cannot see the kingdom of God." Nicodemus asked, "How can a man be born when he is old? Can he enter a second time into his mother's womb and be born?" Jesus answered him, "Unless one is born of water and the Spirit, he cannot enter the kingdom of God." "That which is born of the flesh is flesh, and that which is born of the Spirit is spirit." (JOHN 3:2-8)

So be born. Be born. Be born. And I mean, be born again.

As I already mentioned, like begets like. And God is a Spirit. Then if God is a Spirit, we can only be correctly referred to as spirits. Why? We are God's offspring! The Psalmist told us:

> *I said, "You are gods, and all of you are children of the Most High."*
>
> PSALM 82:6

Jesus corroborated this in John 10:34-35:

> *Jesus answered them, "Is it not written in your law, 'I said. "You are gods"? If He called them gods, to whom the word of God came (and the Scripture cannot be broken).*

So we are transformed into the class of God when the word of God washes us clean, inside-out. Jesus said we must be born of "water" and "the Spirit". The water symbolizes the word of God, while the Spirit symbolises the baptism of the Holy Spirit.

> *That he might sanctify and cleanse it with the washing of water by the word.*
>
> EPHESIANS 5:26

Being born of water is the spiritual process of mind renewal to God's word. See how Paul put it:

> *Do not conform yourselves to the standards of this world, but let God transform you inwardly by a complete change of your mind. Then you will be able to know the will of God.*
>
> ROMANS 12:1 (MSG)

Once we were without, as dogs. But when we became born again, our status changed from that of a dog to a sheep, and then to a lion. The lion status is what qualifies us for a life of signs, but we cannot achieve this status until we learn to renew our mind to God's word.

Concerning the Spirit, the Bible records:

> And being assembled together with them, He (Jesus) commanded them not to depart from Jerusalem, but to wait for the promise of the Father, "which," He said, "You have heard from Me; for John truly baptized with water, but you shall be baptized with the Holy Spirit not many days from now." Therefore when they had come together, they asked Him, saying, "Lord, will You at this time restore the kingdom to Israel?" And He said to them, "It is not for you to know times and seasons which the Father has put in His own authority. But you shall receive power when the Spirit has come upon you; and you shall be witnesses to Me in Jerusalem, and in all Judea and Samaria, and to the end of the earth."

So the essence of "the Spirit" is to empower us. The word baptism is from the original Greek word baptismo, meaning to submerge, soak, temper. The water cleanses us. The Spirit empowers. The water helps with transformation. The Spirit helps with conformation. We are born for transformation; we must not end in deformation. We are created for conformation; we can't afford to die in confusion. It is time we take a stand, a stand for our birthright.

After waiting in the upper room for 120 days, the Holy Spirit finally descended on the disciples, and there was an outbreak of fire. It was a resurgence of divine supernatural empowerment. See how the Bible recorded it in Acts chapter two verses one to four:

When the Day of Pentecost had fully come, they were all with one accord in one place. And suddenly there came a sound from heaven, as of a rushing mighty wind, and it filled the whole house where they were sitting. Then there appeared to them divided tongues, as of fire, and one sat upon each of them. Spirit and began to speak with other tongues as the Spirit gave the utterance.

This is the beauty of new birth. At new birth we have been regenerated.

Friend, if you are not born again, this is your time to be born again. This is your time. This is your season. You will not miss it, in Jesus name!

My little children of whom I travail in birth again until Christ be formed in you.

GALATIANS 4:19

I've come to believe that each of us has a personal calling that's as a unique fingerprint - and that the best way to succeed is to discover what you love and then find a way to offer it to others in the form of service, working hard, and also allowing the energy of the universe to lead you.
OPRAH WINFREY, Talk Show Host

10

BE BRIGHT

"Miracles can be made
but only by sweating."
GIOVANNI AGNELLI, auto executive

To be bright here means to be successful. God has made us the light of the world, and commanded us to shine our lights. Our lives should shine like stars in the midst of a world that has been darkened by sin, corruption and filth. As Christians, we should be living and walking examples of a supreme life in Christ. Proverbs 13:26 told us:

The righteous is more excellent than his neighbour.

God's thought to us as His dear children are to be brighter than the children of this world. Remember how Jesus was at a tender age of twelve? The Bible records that they found him in the temple, sitting in the midst of the teachers, listening to them and asking them questions. And the Bible added that all who heard Him were amazed at His understandingand answers. That was under the New Covenant.Also under the Old Covenant,Daniel and his colleagueswere found to be ten times better than their contemporarieswith their godly lifestyle intact. (Luke 2:46-47;Daniel 1:20)

Daniel was a young Jewishman between eighteen and twenty five yearsold. Along with some other Israelites, Daniel was captured by Nebuchadnezzar the king of Babylonand takento the city of Babylon.As of the time, although Babylon was a greater society than Israel, Nebuchadnezzacould not haveconqueredIsrael,but for the life of compromiseandmediocrityof the Israelites.

While the Israeliteswerebusyliving alife of compromise, crawlingon the ground of mediocrity andstrugglingto get by in life, Nebuchadnezzabesiegedhe nation of Israel, conqueredit and took some Israelitesascaptives.Along with someotheryoungmenof Israel,Danielwasalsotaken captive.Little did Daniel know that his captivity would soonbeturnedaround.

Then, Babylonwas agreat city Under Nebuchadnezzar's reign, Babylonhadbecomethe seatof the world's power, theworld'swisdomandwealth.Under Nebuchadnezzar's reign,Babylonconqueredeveryothersocietyin theworld. The then-known city of Babyloncould be likened to the United Stateof Americaof today but Daniel did not allow himselfto beintimidatedbythis,andinsteadheldon to his valuesof life.

As for these four young men, God gave them knowledge and skill in all literature and wisdom; and Daniel had understanding in all vision and dreams.

Daniel and his colleagues, Shadrach, Meshach, Abednego, were found to be ten times better than all their contemporaries and found to be brighter all the best of Babylonia.

This is the will of God for you and me in Christ Jesus. We are the light of the world. No wonder, Jesus in one of the gospels referred to John the Baptist as a shining light.

Friend, we are created to be better, not to be bordered. Let's set ourselves free.

Come on, arise and shine! It is your turn to shine.

> Make your brain work, It will sweat, but it will improve. It will develop until you become the envy of those around you.
> E. W. KENYON

11

BE BOLD

"Whatever you can do or dream you can, begin it
Boldness has genius power and magic in it"
JOHANN VON GOETHE

You are the righteousness of God in Christ Jesus. Please be bold!

I remember after I gave my life to Christ, we are having a deliverance session in church (not The Elevation Church), and when it got to my turn, my pastor prayed, "Lord, I come against the spirit of timidity."

For some time I didn't get the message but when I eventually did, the pastor himself knew I had gotten the message. Prior to this time, I had been shy, quiet and would hardly utter a word even when asked to speak.

Afterwards, things changed radically I would boldly stand before the congregation to give testimonies, confidently teach the adult Sunday school class give a weekday service exaltation or preach on a Sunday morning service and the entire church would be thrown into a rapturous cheer! My God! It feels good to be bold. It feels godly to be bold. Today I'm as bold as a lion!

The unbelievers are scared as cats. The believers are bold as lions. You are a believer, not an unbeliever. So please be bold. Be bold like a lion. It is part of nature in Christ Jesus.

> *But Daniel purposed in his heart that he would not defile himself with the portion of the king's delicacies, or with the wine which he drank; therefore he requested of the prince of the eunuchs that he might not defile himself.*
>
> DANIEL 1: 8

This takes boldness!

This takes heart!

The bible also gave an account of the audacious faith of Peter and John. In Acts 4:13-14, the Bible records:

> *...when they saw the boldness of Peter and John, and perceived that they were uneducated and untrained men, they marveled. And they realized that they had been with Jesus. And seeing the man who had been healed standing with them, they could say nothing against it.*

You may ask, "How can one operate in boldness?" Let me tell you the trade secret of boldness. It is found in Acts 4:23-31:

And being let go, they went to their own companions and reported all that the chief priests and elders had said to them. So when they heard that, they raised their voice to God with one accord and said: "Lord, You are God, who made heaven and earth and the sea, and all that is in them, who by the mouth of Your servant David have said: 'Why did the nations rage, and the people plot vain things? The kings of the earth took their stand, and the rulers were gathered together against the LORD and against His Christ.' "For truly against Your holy Servant Jesus, whom You anointed, both Herod and Pontius Pilate, with the Gentiles and the people of Israel, were gathered together to do whatever Your hand and Your purpose determined before to be done. Now, Lord, look on their threats, and grant to Your servants that with all boldness they may speak Your word, by stretching out Your hand to heal, and that signs and wonders may be done through the name of Your holy Servant Jesus." And when they had prayed, the place where they were assembled together was shaken; and they were filled with the Holy Spirit, and the spoke the word of God with boldness.

The word of God is our ticket for boldness.

Praying God's word is the fastest track to boldness.

Relying on the help of the Holy Spirit is the factor for boldness.

The disciples searched out the word of God concerning boldness. They prayed the word for boldness, then the Holy Spirit came and equipped them with boldness, and they went about preaching about Jesus with signs, wonders andmiraclesfollowing.

Pleaselocate God'sword that hasto do with boldnessand put pressureon God'sword in prayerfor boldness.Then bebold. Be bold!

Go back to the companythat refusedto give you a job; applyagainto that schoolthat did not giveyou admission; get backto that personthat said he or shecannot marry you, and when you do, make sureyou are bold aslion.

EleanorRooseveltFormer First Ladyof the United States, once asserted,'You gainstrength,courageand confidence by everyexperiencein which you reallystopto look fearin the face.You areableto sayto yourself,'I have lived through this horror. I cantake the next thing that comesalong.'... You must do the thing you think you cannotdo."

Pleasebe bold asa lion. The righteousare bold asa lion. Then you will seesignsand wondersasthe Holy Spirit enablesyouwith divinesupernaturalboldness.

> The righteous ae bold as lion.
> PROVERBS 28:1

12

BE BRAVE

> I learned that courage was not the absence of fear, but the triumph over it. The brave man is not he who does not feel afraid, but he who conquers that fear.
> NELSON MANDELA, Civil Rights leader

To be brave here simply means to be strong, courageous and confident. These are core attributes of the lion. A lion is strong, courageous and confident. As lions after the order of the Lion of the Tribe of Judah, we have been circuitously wired up to be the same.

> There are three things which are majestic in pace, yes, four are stately in walk: A lion, which is mighty among beasts and does not turn away from any.
>
> PROVERBS 30:30

In the time of Daniel in Babylon, after the announcement was made that no one should pray to any other God except the golden image, Daniel simply opened his window and prayed to God as his custom was. That takes courage. That takes confidence.

One of the characteristics of a lion is bravery. God expects us to be brave. To be brave means to be strong, or if you prefer, courageous. It is obvious that we are in the dangerous days because of all the dogged, devilish and diabolical roaring, raging and ranting that we see and hear around us. But, thank God! The dangerous days are also the greatest day for God's people. Why? It will feature an unusual release of supernatural strength, and culminate in the release of divine courage. I can hear the trumpet sounding louder than ever:

"Doing the Impossible is the destiny of the brave. So be brave. Don't bury your destiny"

In Psalm 110:1-3, the Psalmist said:

> The LORD said unto my Lord, "Sit at My right hand, till I make Your enemy Your footstool." The LORD shall send the rod of Your strength out of Zion.

Rule in the midst of your enemies!

"The rod of thy strength" connotes strength. That kind of strength was depicted in Samson. That is what we see in the record of Judges:

> Then went Samson down to Timnah with his father and mother, and came to the vineyards of Timnah. Now to his surprise, a young lion came roaring him. And the Spirit of the Lord came mightily upon him, and he tore the lion apart

as one would have torn apart a young goat, though he had nothing in his hand. But he did not tell his father or his mother what he had done.

JUDGES 14:5-6

Isn't this incredible?

The young lion roared, but Samson defeated him. Samson was a one-man army. Nations were frightened of Samson, and he was the strength of the then-known Israelite nation. He destroyed the lion as though it was a chicken. Samson broke chains as though they were strings of thread. He also uprooted the gate of a whole city with its posts single-handedly and climbed up a mountain, carrying it, as though it had been a wooden door frame. All this was done by the instrumentality of strength.

> Courage is not limited to the battlefield. The real tests of courage are much quieter. They are the inner tests, like enduring pain when the room is empty or standing alone when you're misunderstood. CHARLES SWINDOLL

13

BE BOUNTIFUL

> There is no passion to be found in playing small,
> in settling for a life that is less than the
> one you are capable of living
> NELSON MANDELA
> 11th President of South Africa

The righteous shall flourish as a branch
PROVERBS 11:28 (KJV)

In Revelation 5:11-12, the Bible says:

> *And I looked, and I heard the voice of many angels round about the throne, the living creatures and the elders; and the number of them was ten thousand times ten thousand times and thousands of thousands, Saying with a loud voice, "Worthy is the Lamb that was slain to receive power and riches and wisdom and strength and honour and glory and blessing!"*

This is our redemptive package in Christ.

This is what salvation is all about.

Come on, friend, its bounty time!

See all that Jesus received for us at redemption. Friend, you are born for riches, not ridicule. You are born of power, not weakness. You are born of wisdom, not foolishness. You are born of strength, not stagnation. You are born for honour, not for horror. You are born for glory, not groaning. You are born for blessing not curses. For you to be alive and living without these things that Jesus has freely given to us at redemption is a disgrace on salvation. No wonder, David the lion cried, "The young lions lack and suffer hunger; but those who seek the LORD shall not lack any good thing. (Psalm 34:10)

I remember the insightful story of a landlord shared by Bishop David Oyedepo. The man had a tenant who had some problems. Then when even paying house rent became a problem for the tenant, the landlord directed him to go to Winners Chapel because he believed the people that attended the church didn't have problems as they are always smiling. So the man started attended Winners Chapel, and things started turning around for him. Another tenant also had some problems so the landlord told him to also go to Winners Chapel. The second man too went and things started turning around for him. Then another man also had some problems and the landlord said to him, "Please go to Winners Chapel. When two of my tenants had issues, I directed them to the church and they are doing well today. May be you too should go there." Then the third man also went, gave his life to Christ and things started turning around for him. Then and later, the man said to himself, "If I can be sending people to this church and their lives are getting better, I think I better go there too." So the man went and today he is a Satellite Fellowship leader in the church. People would question your Christianity because you are not flourishing. So please start flourishing like a palm tree. That is the heritage of the children of God.

> *A fire devours before them, and behind them a flame burns; the land is like the Garden of Eden before them, and behind them a desolate wilderness, surely nothing shall escape them.*
> JOEL 2:3

What a colourful army!

It is not the will of God for us to be poor. As a young man growing up, poor fellows were always described with the simile, as poor as a church rat. But thank God, today the reverse is the case. The church rat is now fat and flourishing. Why? Church folks are gaining unusual insights into God's present-day prophetic agenda for them. Is this not wonderful?

This Bible authenticates the status of this army as a super wealthy army. They will be like Adam who was so wealthy that he did not own just a pool but rivers.

Poverty is not a friend; it is an enemy. Let us fight it. And of course, it is not enough for us to conquer our enemy called poverty; we are also required to go all out to embrace our friend called plenty. I hear the sound of abundance; Its a shower of blessing and it is going to come as a deluge. You will not miss your place in it.

Please say this out loud:

I am born of power, therefore power I will have!

I am born of riches, therefore riches I will have!

I am born of wisdom, therefore wisdom I will have!

I am born of strength, therefore strength I will have!

I am born of honour, therefore honour I will have!

I am born of glory, therefore glory I will have!

I am born of blessing, therefore blessing I will have!

Contentment comes not so much
from great wealth as from few wants.
EPICTETUS, Philosopher

14

BE BIG

> As long as you're going to be thinking anyway, think big.
> DONALD TRUMP, Real Estate Magnate

We are in the age of greatness in the Church. Greatness distinguishes Christianity from all other religions. When Christianity lacks power, it is reduced to a mere religious activity. I hear people say America is the world power. That is the greatest mistake of all ages. The Bible does not tell us that the government shall be upon the shoulder of America. What the Bible tells us is that the government shall be upon the shoulder of the Church (Isaiah 4:6).

It is the will of God for all His creations to be the best. God created the birds to fly so he put wings on birds. God created the fishes to swim so He put fins and gills into the fishes. God created man to be the best so God put the best into man. This is what we see in the life of Adam, the forefather of mankind. Before the fall, Adam operated in the frequency of God, and Adam was at his best.

> *Adam, before he sinned, was the world's greatest. Everything about him was fantastic. His body was in its best form, hence there was no need for medical drugs or alternative medical drugs; all the herbs then were for food. His mind was the best. He single-handedly named all the animals without a single mistake. He had the heart of a lion. Every beast naturally submitted to his authority. Doubtlessly, Adam's life was fascinating. But after sin, his life was shattered. It was a tragedy. No wonder, Paul admitted, "All have sinned and come short of the greatness of God."*
>
> (Romans 3:23 Paraphrase Mine)

People like Daniel must have learned from the fall of the first man. Everyone was grounded in mediocrity because of their defilement. "But Daniel purposed in his heart that he would not defile himself." (Daniel 1:8) Thus, Daniel was distinct because of his dedication to God the Source of greatness.

Start Small…

In the King James Version of the book of Job chapter 8 verse 7, the richest man in his day once advised:

> *Though thy beginning was small, yet thy latter end should greatly increase.*

Success starts from the beginning; Healing starts from the beginning; Victory starts from the beginning. In fact, friend, everything that is good and right starts from the beginning.

I remember just after secondary school, I sat for my University Matriculation Examination, and waited for my name to be shortlisted. Finally the results were released, but following up on my admission process became an uphill task. I couldn't get financial support from my dad because had become a born-again Christian, and he was not interested in sponsoring my educational pursuits. In addition, I had gained admission to a polytechnic institution, I didn't quite appreciate polytechnic, and would have preferrred to have gone to a university. Today my first degree is from a polytechnic.

Oh, yes! I couldn't get what I wanted, but I started with what I had. As I am writing this book right now, I don't just have a first degree I also have an MBA. But I started first and I started small.

Start small. Success starts small. That is the reason it is called success. success is succession.

…End Big!

Thy latter end should greatly increase.

When we know our root, doing the impossible comes naturally to us.

A Lion is big. And because you belong to the lion family, being big is your portion. The lion family is a big family. It will be disgrace to your family if you are not big. Why? God already promised us a big life in Jeremiah 30:19:

I will multiply them, and they shall not be few; I will also glorify them, and they shall not be small.

Friend, you are born for multiplication, not mourning. So sit up! You are created to be glorified, not to be grounded. So go get it! It is not the will of God for us to be few. Neither is remaining small His plan for us. That is why David cried, "I am small and despised." (Psalms 119:114) Have you ever seen a lion been despised before? No! It is time we awaken the sleeping lion within you!

Let's digress a little with the story of David. At a very crucial time in the history of Israel when the Israelite army was faced with the Philistine-Goliath problem that seemed practically impossible to surmount, it took David, a man with a lion heart to stop the cruel confrontation of the enemy

This is incredible!

It takes heart.

Remember what David said? "Let no man's heart fail." Why? The one with the lion heart has come on the scene. So the enemy roaring like a lion has no alternative, than to quit like the young lion and the bear

Though David was small at this time and Goliath, the Philistine despised him for being so. What Goliath, the Philistine did not realise was that David had his root in God. And when God is on your side, the giants must fall!

PART THREE

3

Taking Your
Lion Shae

The first part of success is "Get-to-it-iveness"; the second part of success is "Stick-to-it-iveness"

ORISON SWETT MARDEN, Editor, Success Magazine

15

LOCATE YOUR LION ROOT

> Knowing thyself is the
> height of wisdom
> SOCRATES

In this chapter I will like to release the blessing upon your life by asking God to make you a man of Psalm chapter one verses one to three. But before then, I will like to share few things with you.

In Revelation 5:4-5, John cried:

> *So I wept much, because no one was found worthy to open and read the scroll, or to look at it. But one of the elders said to me, "Do not weep. Behold, the Lion of the tribe of Judah, the Root of David, has prevailed to open the scroll and to loose its seven seals."*

In Revelation 22:16, the Jesus, the Lion of the tribe of Judah Himself declared:

I Jesus… am the root.

The Lord is saying:

" I Am the Root, not a root. I Am your Root, not the devil."

Jesus said, "I am the root." Jesus, the Lion of the tribe of Judah, is the root. When you carry this mentality, no devil will be able to harass, molest or embarrass you with any form of mediocrity. David had this mentality. So when a lion came to attack his father's sheep, he went after the lion and slew him.

Dr. Myles Munroe, a very notable author, shared an insight on this context that I think can help us appreciate it better. He said:

In 1976, I was a student at a renowned university, and one of my major areas of study was fine art. In this course of study, we had to produce paintings, stone sculptures, drawings, and artwork in a variety of media. I loved the stone and wood sculpture work and learned many lessons from the experience. However, one of the most significant lessons I learned concerned the principles of source and resource and their relation to purpose and potential. These lessons have cultivated and formed the foundation of my understanding of and my philosophy of life.

On two occasions, I set about working on a wood and stone sculpture project and chose my raw materials from discarded pieces of trees and stones. After labouring many hours following the design I had developed, the day came when I was finally finished and proud of the results. When I submitted my project to the professor, I obtained an A and was successful in fulfilling my requirement for graduation. I was so proud of my sculptures that I took them home with me and placed them in a very prominent place in my apartment.

A year later, however, something happened that changed the life of my sculptures forever. I decided to clean the wooden sculpture and wax the stonework. As I picked up the wooden piece to shine the results of my hardwork, part of the wood stayed on the table and the other part came off in my hands. My heart sank as the bottom of the figure then gave way and fell apart right before my eyes.

Deeply shocked at this turn of events, I moved the stone sculpture and wondered if the same thing would happen. As I rubbed lightly with the cloth, the stone began to come apart like dust. With great disappointment and despair, I had to accept the reality that all my work had been in vain and that the rest of my artwork was destined for disintegration. Today both pieces are only memories, but I cherish more the lesson this experience taught me. Here is the greatest wisdom I gained from the wood and stone sculpture:

1. The nature of the composition of the source material determines the nature of the composition of the product made or produced from it.

2. Whatever is in the source is in the product.

3. The strength and durability of the source determines the durability of the product made from it.

4. The ability of the product is only as good as the ability of its source.

5. If the source is porous and weak, then the product will be porous and weak.

6. The key principle is that a thing consists of the same components and consistency as that from which it came.

In other words, it is our destiny to do the impossible But to do the impossible, we must constantly align ourselves at the right angle to the principles of destiny or we stand the risk of ending in devastation, like Reuben, Jacob's first born.

> *Reuben, you are my firstborn, my might and the beginning of my strength, the excellence of dignity and the excellence of power. Unstable as water, you shall not excel, because you went up to your father's bed, then defiled you it - he went up to my couch.*
>
> GENESIS 49:3-4

Reuben did not align himself to the principles of destiny so he ended up in devastation In spite of the excellency of strength, and of power that was exhibited in his life, Reuben did not excel! Oh, no! That will not be your portion.

Why do you think Reuben ended up in mediocrity? Verse 4 tells us:

> Unstable as water, you shall not excel, because you went up to you father's bed, there defiled you out - he went up to my couch.

And what do you think could have taken him away from excellence into mediocrity? Isaiah 33:6 tells us:

> Wisdom and knowledge will be the stability of your times, and the strength of salvation; the fear of the LORD is His treasure.

Today many people around the world are living with the Reubenite syndrome. They know that it is their destiny to do the impossible; they even know that they have all they need to do the impossible. But because they refuse to take the right steps, like Reuben, they end up in devastation, or end up being destitute. What a malady!

But this is your hour of recovery. You are a man of destiny not a destitute. So wake up and recover yourself!

"Unstable as water." Hot today cold tomorrow; Cold today hot tomorrow. In fact, Jesus described this condition as being lukewarm…neither cold nor hot. Jesus said He will spew such out.

Be still. Be stable. That's the cheapest way to growing your lion root.

In Proverbs 12:12, Solomon said:

The wicked covet the catch of evil men, but the root of the righteous yields fruit.

Your root dictates your fruit. In my culture, parents tell their children that are about to embark on a long journey to always remember the son (or daughter) of who they are. I have heard my mother say it many times, and I can still vividly remember her saying to my sister over the telephone. In other words, they mean to say: always remember your root. Your root always comes first, and a proof of the quality and strength of your root is in the manifestation of your fruit.

If this is your root, then prove it by your fruits. It is only fools that will doubt your proofs.

When we know our root, doing the impossible comes naturally to us.

> The source is the authority and
> sustainer of the product
> DR MYLES MUNROE

16

WANT YOUR LION SHARE?

Think you can, think you can't; either
way, you'll be right"
HENRY FORD, Industrialist

At first, as a student, I wanted freedom only for myself, the transitory freedoms of being able to stay out at night, read what I pleased, and go where I chose. Later as a younger man in Johannesburg I yearned for the basic and the honourable freedom of achieving my potential, of earning my keep, of marrying and having a family – the freedom not to be obstructed in a lawful life. But I then slowly saw that not only was I not free, but my brothers and sisters were not free. that is when my hunger for my own freedom became the greater hunger for the freedom of my people.

It was this desire for the freedom of my people to live their lives with dignity and self-respect that animated my life, that transformed a frightened young man into a bold one, that drove a law-abiding attorney to become a criminal, that turned a family-loving husband *into a man without a home…I am no more virtuous or self sacrificing than the next man, but I found that I could not ever enjoy the poor and limited freedoms I was allowed when I knew my people were not free.*

This is the story of a thirsty soul; the story of a hungry man. Obviously, Nelson Mandela did not achieve destiny by chance; he achieved destiny by choice. So many people believe that life should be left to chances "Whatever would be would be," they say I do not believe that life should be left to chances I believe we must be deliberate about what we want from life, like Nelson Mandela was.

In Ezekiel 34:1-30, the prophet said:

> And the word of the LORD came to me saying, "Son of man, prophesy against the shepherds of Israel prophesy and say to them, "Thus says the LORD GOD to the shepherds: "Woe to the shepherds of Israel who feed themselves Should not the shepherds feed the flocks? You eat the fat and clothe yourselves with the wool; you slaughter the fatlings, but you do not feed the flock…therefore thus says the Lord GOD to them…I will make a covenant of peace with them and cause wild beasts to cease from the land; and they will dwell safely in the wilderness and sleep in the woods I will them and the places all around My hill a blessing and I will cause shower to come down in their season, there shall be showers of blessing Then the trees of the field shall yield their fruit, and the earth shall yield her increase They shall be safe in their land; and they shall know that I am the LORD, when I have broken the bands of their yoke and delivered them from the hands of those

whoenslave them And they shall no longer be a prey for the
nations, nor shall beasts of the land devour them, but they
shall dwell safely, and no one shall make them afraid. I will
raise up for them a garden of renown, and they shall no longer
be consumed with hunger in the land, nor bear the shame of the
Gentiles anymore. Thus they shall know that I, the LORD
their God, am with them, and they, the house of Israel, are
My people, says the Lord GOD.

The young lion in our story had to make a change across
the river to its true self; a lasting change that could occur
only when it took place in the spirit of the mind. Without
this metamorphosis, no amount of training, study, or
education can transform a sheep into a lion.

The young lion's attitude was that of a desperate soul. In
essence, a converted attitude is the key to a transformed
life. Until this attitude change happens, the lion will still
think, act, respond, and live like a sheep instead of the king
of the jungle. How desperately do you want your Lion's
Share? David the king, was an example of a desperate soul.
In Psalm 63:1-3, he cried:

O God, You are my God; early will I seek You; my soul
thirsts for You; my flesh longs for You in a dry and thirsty land
where there is no water. So as I have looked for You in the
sanctuary, to see Your power and Your glory

Spiritual hunger is a major requirement to receive your
lion share. David had an unbridled appetite, and his
spiritual taste buds were super active. However, he also
realized that God is the ultimate source of excellence. So

David continued to seek God. He knew that if he could catch God's favour, he had caught something good.

How hungry are you for excellence? In which area of your life do you really desire excellence? Dr. Mike Murdock says, "Pursuit is the proof of desire." If your quest for excellence is genuine, you would develop a spiritual hunger for it.

The Thirst Factor

How hungry are you? How thirsty are you? How desperate are the African nations for developed economies? When will our Lagos city be comparable to New York in terms of architectural infrastructure? How hungry are our leaders for true democracy with its attendant dividends? How hungry is the Church for an experience of God's healing power like in the 50s?

> *When the poor and needy seek water, and there is none, and their tongue faileth for thirst, I the LORD will hear them, I the God of Israel will not forsake them. I will open rivers in high places, and fountains in the midst of the valleys: I will make the wilderness a pool of water, and the dry land springs of water*

> ISAIAH 41:17-18

God is saying, "I will pour water upon the thirsty." But you must be thirty first. You must apply the thirst factor.

Spielberg is one of the greatest film producers in the history of the world. From the age of thirteen, Spielberg knew he wanted to be a film director. His life changed when he took a tour of Universal Studios one afternoon when he was seventeen years old. The tour did not quite make it to the sound stages where all the action was, so Spielberg, knowing his result, took a step. He snuck off by himself to watch the filming of a real movie. He ended up meeting the head of Universal's editorial department, who talked with him for an hour and expressed an interest in Spielberg's film.

The next day, Spielberg put on a suit, brought along his father's briefcase, loaded with only a sandwich and two candy bars, and returned to the lot as if he belonged there. He strode purposefully past the gate guard. He found an abandoned trailer and, using some plastic letters, wrote Steven Spielberg, Director, on the door. Then he went on to spend his summer meeting directors, writers, editors, lingering at the edges of the world he craved, learning from every conversation, observing and developing more and more acumen about what worked in moviemaking.

At last, at age twenty, after becoming a regular on the lot, Spielberg showed Universal a modest film he had put together, and he was offered a seven-year contract to direct a TV series. At the age of thirty-six, he has become the most successful film maker in history.

What you do not expect, you cannot experience. Every great encounter begins with a longing of the spirit and a thirst of the soul. This is what we have in Psalm 63:1-2:

Excellence is real. It is our covenant redemption heritage.

Friend, we must get what rightful belongs to us. We must go after excellence with all spiritual alacrity doing all that we need to do to get it. We must not sell short; Esau did, and he wept bitterly for it. But tears could not bring back what had been lost. It was pathetic.

That will not be your portion!

Ask the LORD for rain in the time of the latter rain. The LORD will make flashing clouds; He will give them showers of rain, grass in the field for everyone.

ZECHARIAH 10:1

Be glad then you children of Zion, and rejoice in the LORD your God; For He has given you the former rain faithfully and He will cause the rain to come down for you–the former rain, and the latter rain in the first month. The threshing floor shall be full of wheat, and the vats shall overflow with new wine and oil. So I will restore to you the years that the swarming locust has eaten, the crawling locust the consuming locust, and the chewing locust, My great army which I sent among you. You shall eat in plenty and be satisfied, and praise the name of the LORD your God, who had dealt wondrously with you, and My people shall never be put to shame.

JOEL 2:23-26

The question isn't who is going to let me; it's who is going to stop me.
AYN RAND

17

RUB MIND
WITH THE LIONS

A man wrapped up in himself
makes a very small bundle.
BENJAMIN FRANKLIN, Mentor

Iron sharpens iron. Remember the story of the lion cub? When the old lion came and all the sheep fled for their lives, the lion cub simply wagged its tail and joined the lion's company Of course, the lion could not have done that without a transformed mind.

The lion cub had rubbed minds with the sheep for years, and I believe as a result, the mentality of the lion cub must have been conditioned over and over again to live as a sheep For example it must have been eating grass when it was destined to be eating flesh. I mean, imagine the lion cub bleating instead of roaring. Thus, the lion cub must have kept the wrong company for years.

Right company is required for right living. Right association is required for positive manifestation. Iron sharpens iron, says King Solomon, the wisest man that ever lived.

Like Stephen Covey prescribed in his best-selling book, The Seven habits of Highly Effective People, to be highly effective, we need to constantly and consistently sharpen our saw. But we need the right sharpener if we must get the right results. "Iron sharpens iron."

I read a story about Richard Templer. I trust it will help us to appreciate the concept of right company from a robust perspective:

When I first became a managing director of a company I almost forgot this Rule. I carried on managing as if I was a senior manager. But sales weren't going as well I would have liked. I was organizing corporate sales and couldn't get to talk to the right people. I read somewhere that kings only talk to kings. I became a king (substitute "managing director" for "king" and you'll see what I mean). Immediately doors which previously had been closed, opened and sales exceeded my expectations.

If you are going to be a king in the future you had better start practicing now. Watch how anyone senior to you does things. The way they answer the phone, talk to staff, what they wear, what paper they read, how they get to work, what they do at work and how they do it.

I recently met a managing director of a very large company and I was seriously impressed with how friendly and informal he was with his staff—who obviously adored him

– and how genuinely relaxed he seemed. That is until we came to negotiate, when he was obviously totally up on his job and had facts and figures at his fingertips in a second. I watched him because he is my next step, if you like. He is my "one of them."

In Acts 4:13-14, the Bible records:

> …when they saw the boldness of Peter and John, and perceived that they were unlearned and ignorant men, they marvelled and they took knowledge of them, that they had been with Jesus. And beholding the man which was healed standing with them, they could say nothing against it.
> ROMANS 8:28-39

By associating with Jesus, Peter and John had begun to act, think and look like Jesus. They had successfully rubbed minds with the Lion of the tribe of Judah, and they were succeeding and dominating their world as a result of this association.

How then do you rub minds? You can rub minds through several ways.

#1   Rub Minds By Reading

Give attention to reading…

I Timothy 4:13

A wise man said unless you change the books and the company you keep, in five years from today you'll be the same person you are today. People either rise or get relegated by what they exposed their minds to.

People that read don't get ruined. Readers are rulers. Until you start reading, you may never rule. Readers rule the world. Remember Daniel, a prisoner that later became a Prime Minister in a foreign land. In Daniel chapter 9 verse 2, this Prime Minister said, "I, Daniel understood by books."

Thomas Edison, notable scientist asserted, "Genius is 1 per cent inspiration, and 99 per cent perspiration." Friend, before inspiration is perspiration. Let's perspire. Let's read. That is one of the ways to expose your mind for limitless exploits.

#2 Rub Minds Through Research

You search the Scriptures, for in them you think you have eternal life; and these are they which testify of Me.

John 5:39

Albert Einstein, a German-born physicist who developed the theory of relativity, was a dropout in high school but he moved beyond that into greatness by asking quality questions. In the process of asking himself thought-provoking questions, Einstein postulated his renowned theory of relativity. He once said, "The important thing is not to stop questioning. Curiosity has its own reason for existing. One cannot help but be in awe when he contemplates the mysteries of eternity, of life, of the marvelous structure of reality. It is enough if one tries to comprehend a little of this mystery everyday. Never lose a holy curiosity."

By doing extensive research and learning from how other people succeeded, you can rub mind with the lions. Dr. Mike Murdock once shared how he bought a little book for $84. Then a young man with him said, "I cannot believe you bought a book for $84." He replied, "Son, I did not. I bought a man's life. What took him 70 years to learn, I will know in two hours."

This is a man that understands what it means to do a diligent search.

#3 Rub Minds Through Rapport

As iron sharpens iron, so a man sharpens the countenance of his friend.

PROVERBS 27:18

Like I quoted a wise man earlier, you will be the person you are today in five years time except you change the company you keep. Moses had a rapport with Jethro. Elisha had a rapport with Elijah. Esther enjoyed a rapport with Mordecai. Ruth appreciated her rapport with Naomi. The twelve disciples had a rapport with Jesus. Timothy had a rapport with Paul. Benny Hinn had a rapport with Katherin Khulma. Manaseh Jordan has a rapport with Benny Hinn. The big question to ask is: Who do you have a rapport with?

Do you remember that as soon as the lion cub saw the lion,

it wagged its tail and went straight ahead to be with the lion? Do you want to rub mind with the lions? Do you want to reign with them? Then stop flocking and feeding with the sheep.

In Acts 4:13-14, the Bible records an insightful:

> ...when they saw the boldness of Peter and John, and perceived that they were unlearned and ignorant men, they marvelled; and they took knowledge of them, that they had been with Jesus. And beholding the man which was healed standing with them, they could say nothing against it."

#4   Rub Minds Through A Ride

> *As in water face answereth to face, so the heart of man to man.*
> PROVERBS 27:19 (KJV)

Michael Faraday the British 19th century inventor and electrical pioneer was an appentice in a printing shop. At the age of 14, he left school and started apprenticeship at a local book binder. In his spare time he was an avid reader of scientific concepts.

In 1812, at the age of 20 he received some tickets for a series of lectures by an eminent scientist, Sir Humphrey Davy. After the lecture, Michael sent Sir Humphrey a 300-page document notes on the lecture. Pleased by the act, Sir Humphrey rode on horseback to look for Michael so as to employ him as his lab assistant.

Later, Michael rose to become a Fullerian Professor of

Chemistry at the royal Institution of Great Britain, a position which made him to become the envy of other scientists as well. His greatest achievement was the development of electro-magnetism and electricity in 1821. But Michael had to ride on the achievements of Sir Humphrey first.

My mother said to me "if you become a soldier you 'll be a general; if you become a monk you'll end up as the Pope." Instead, I became a painter and wound up as Picasso.
PABLO PICASSO

18

TAKE YOUR LION SHARE – NOW!

Apostle Paul, admonishing Timothy in his letter to Timothy said:

This charge I commit to you, son Timothy according to the prophecies previously made concerning you, that by them you may wage the good warfare.

1 TIMOTHY 1:18

"A lion which is mighty among beasts and does not turn away from any"

This is our destiny. This is what doing the impossible is all about! Friend, we are in for a contest! We must not mistaken this for a ceremony Let's stop playing church. Let's stop playing membership. Let's stop fantasizing and face the facts. It is a contest. We must contend in this battle if we are to realise our dreamed victory.

Excellence is not by dictation. It is by decision. And part of this decision is a resolute decision to fight. Your destiny is a function of your personal decision. Decision is sequel to distinction. David's decision to destroy Goliath of the Philistines was what ultimately put him on the golden throne of the Israelites.

Taking your lion share is a fight, let us not mistaken it for fun. David understood this very well. No wonder, he cried, "You prepare a table before me in the presence of my enemies; You anoint my head with oil; My cup runs over" (Psalm 23:5). That means, the devil was there contesting the destiny of David despite the enormity of power upon his life to fulfil his destiny as a king. The time has finally come for us to make our decisions – quality decisions – if we must see the determination of the enemy destroyed. The battle is now, and it is tense! It is rugged! It is dogged! But we must fight it.

God is blowing His trumpet:

"Fight! Or, you'll become a casualty."

How do we respond to God's trumpet call?

First, we need to decide to do the battle to take our lion share. Your lion share may be good health, financial boom, peaceful home, academic excellence, or what have you. Secondly we must understand that the battle we are fighting has been won in our favour even before we began. Thirdly, we must understand that we have been given all power and authority in heaven and on earth to repeat the victory that has been won in our favour over satan and his cohorts. Lastly we must take authority by exercising our God-given authority over the enemy as we contend with him in battle.

Nothing just happens, things are made to happen. You will have to make your dream happen. You will have to make marital bliss happen. You will have to make your admission into an institution of higher learning happen. You will have to pin the enemy to the ground. So roll up your sleeves, flex your muscles and get into the ring. As long as you do not leave, slack off or play hook, you will be too much for the enemy that he will be afraid to even fight in the ring with you. This is what I call the concept of repeat victory – duplicating the victory of Jesus over satan and sin over again and again.

Even our God is a fighter. Genesis 1:2-3 says:

> *The earth was without form, and void; and darkness was on the face of the deep. And the Spirit of God was hovering over the face of the waters. Then God said, "let there be light"; and there was light.*

Then, in verse 31:

> *Then God saw everything that He had made, and indeed it was very good.*

Excellent! Isn't it?

God had a problem just like any man can, but God did not sit on the fence, fold his arms and watch things happen. No! He struggled against the situation until possibility came out of impossibility.

I remember a vision that I received from God in 1993. I was standing alone in an open field. Then, having perceived what was about to happen to me, I started praying to God for help. Momentarily and spontaneously, a certain being— black from the crown of his head to the soul of his feet— jumped over me from nowhere. And we began to fight. We fought and fought until I was able to back slam him. Then, suddenly another being who looked exactly like the one I had earlier fought with, appeared from nowhere with a fork in his hand, withdrew this hideous being away from me. Then, I stood to my feet and began to say "Thank You, Jesus! Thank You, Jesus!" I believe God showed me this vision in order to prepare me for the battles that lie ahead in the future.

From the outset, people have had to fight to do the impossible. This, I believe, is the trend that will continue in the history of humanity until Jesus comes. Adam was confronted with this fight in the Garden of Eden. The devil came, fought and won because Adam allowed him to. Thus, Adam lost his God-given authority, an authority that rightfully belonged to him.

It was a tragedy. But it didn't end there.

The last Adam, Jesus, came, fought the devil, and defeated him totally to restore back to us our God-given authority that was once lost through the first Adam. That's what Matthew 28:18 told us:

> And Jesus came and spoke to them, saying, "All authority has been given to Me in heaven and on earth."

Jesus recovered the lost authority from satan to restore it back to you and me. You may like to ask, "How did Jesus restore the authority back to man?" Luke 10:19 tells us:

> Behold, I (Jesus) give you the authority (as it was given to Me) to trample on serpents and scorpions, and over all the power of the enemy, and nothing shall by any means hurt you.
>
> LUKE 10:19 (Paraphrase Mine)

Remember, Adam was given complete authority at creation. God created man as male and female. "Then God blessed them, and God said to them, "Be fruitful and multiply; fill the earth and subdue it; have dominion over the fish of the sea, over the birds of the air, and over every living thing that moves on earth." (Genesis 1:28)

The word dominion here is from its original Greek translational some an complete authority. At creation, God gave man dominion. In the beginning the authority of Adam was unquestionable, unchallengeable and unbeatable. Not even satan, the serpent could question his authority. Satan was the serpent in the Garden of Eden, and after he tempted Adam, Adam lost his dominion. We must locate the map of Eden and retrace our footsteps and return home. We have sojourned too long in Egypt under the oppressive power of the Egyptian Pharaoh. It is time to go back to Eden.

And when we get to Eden, the Land of Promise, we are not going to hang around, folding our hands, watching things happen. We will trample every serpent and scorpion and adder and cobra and every power of the enemy. We will exercise our authority to the letter; and we will do it with a possessor's mentality.

> Rise, take your journey, and cross over the River Arnon. Look, I have given into your hand Sihon the Amorite, king of Heshbon, and his land. Begin to possess it, and engage him in battle.
>
> DEUTERONOMY 2:24

Taking your lion share is essentially a spiritual battle, and we cannot afford to take it lightly or wrongly identify it as a natural issue. The present spiritual dryness in the church should concern us. The present economic downturn should get us worried.

We must not watch our family get torn apart. We must not watch our children go wayward right under our noses. We must not watch our dreams of possibilities go down the drain. We must fight now, or never. Though the battle has been declared in our favour, we still have to partake in effectivewarfareto secureour victory. The fightersarethe winners.Until wefight, wecannotwin.

Our doubts ar traitors, And make us lose the good we oft might win, By faring to attempt.
WILLIAMS SHAKESPEE

PART FOUR

4

Prevail
As A Lion

An army of lions led by
a sheep will be defeated
by an army of sheep led
by a lion.

OLD PROVERB

19

SEASON
OF CHANGE

Some men see things as they are,
and say 'why?' I dream of things
that never were, and say, 'why not?'
GEORGE BERNARD SHAW

In Psalm 87:7, the Lord declares:

All my springs are in you.

I am very glad to announce that the end-time church is programmed for an untold move of God. It will be an untold divine movement because it is going to be strange to the sight and hearing of many.

The body of Christ will constitute the foremost world leaders. The people of God will take the lead in every human field of endeavour. The church will constitute the world pacesetters. Folks in the church will set an unusual pace in every sector of the global economy. While the world is still struggling to catch up with one move, the Church will be setting the next one. The entire world is still trying to understand how the largest single Christian gathering was held in Lagos, Nigeria. They are still trying to comprehend how the largest single church auditorium was built in Lagos, Nigeria when all the buildings of the Covenant universe were built. And this divine revival is going to come in a grand style. The saints of God will be succeeding at will.

That is why Paul said:

> But as it is written: "Eye has not seen, nor ear heard, nor have entered into the heart of man the things which God has prepared for those who love Him.
>
> 1 CORINTHIANS 2:9

It is going to be a mind-blowing experience. The who-is-who of our generation will locate their root in the church. The move of the Spirit that has never been witnessed before will begin to find practical expression in the body of Christ. By that time, the move of God in the 1950s, as it were, will be considered a mere tale. The end-time church will be exploding in so much power that the devil will cry out loud, "Lord, let your kingdom come!" The church, I perceive, is a heavenly mechanism set up to rewrite the history of the earth.

You will not be a misfit. I see the glory of this on-coming move resting upon you. Jesus was a sensitive leader. One moment, He told His disciples, "Don't carry a pulse, you won't need it." Another moment He said, "Gather all the money you can and buy yourselves swords." Jesus had an understanding of what it meant to be divinely guided. He knew that for every new move, there would be a new instruction. He understood the principle of divine direction very well because He started it.

For every new move, there is a new instruction. Preparation precedes manifestation. As we are about to enter a new chapter of God's plan for us, and take up the responsibility as custodians of God's new move, I believe we need to prepare ourselves so that we don't crumble under the weight of this imminent move.

> *I will open rivers in desolate heights and fountains in the midst of the valleys; I will make the wilderness a pool of water, and dry land springs of water*
>
> ISAIAH 41:18

Still on God's present-day prophetic agenda for the church, as the world is crying, "There is cast-down", the church will be saying "There is an uplifting." God is going to convert the wisdom of this world to foolishness. The mighty men of this world will be reduced to mere men. The wise men of this world will be reduced to weary men. But the church will emerge the economic power of this world. The Church will emerge the powerhouse of this world.

Friend, get ready to leave a mark on the sands of your days. Get ready for maximum impact. Daniel was a revolutionary. In spite of all odds in the then-known Babylon, he still climbed his way to the top.

Daniel had an understanding of the move of God's move. "Then this Daniel distinguished himself above the governors and satraps, because an excellent spirit was in him; and the king gave thought to set him over the whole realm" (Daniel 6:3). Thus, Daniel emerged an envy of his generation.

> *The Spirit Himself bears witness with our spirit that we are the children of God, and if children, then heirs—heirs of God and joint heirs with Christ, if indeed we suffer with him, that we may also be glorified together. For I consider that the sufferings of this present time are not worthy to be compared with the glory which shall be revealed in. For the earnest expectation of the creation eagerly waits for the revealing of the sons of God. For the creation was subjected to futility, not willingly, but because of Him who subjected it in hope; because the creation itself also will be delivered from the bondage of corruption into the glorious liberty of the children of God. For we know that the whole creation groans and labors with birth pangs together until now.*
>
> ROMANS 8:16-22

Friend, God wants to put some revolution in your life, let Him do it. However, the Bible says the Spirit of excellence in Daniel was the secret of his outstanding success. What is the Spirit of excellence? What is the ministry of the Spirit of excellence? What qualifies one for an encounter with the Spirit of excellence? In this chapter, we shall find answers.

In 1904, a meeting (of the London Society of Engineers) held that it was impossible for a piece of metal to fly in the air. The engineers came up with a lot of reasons to buttress their assertion. But two boys of the same father, the Wright brothers, sat up and said, "That's their own. We are not part of their association. Our own is to get our plan worked out." And so they started working out their plan. And by 1910, despite all the sanctions of the scientific authority, the first piece of metal went up in the air. This is what a revelation can do. Revolution is revelation-provoked.

In the 1950s, the baptism of the Holy Spirit was such a strange thing that everybody marvelled at it. But in this era, the church is going to manifest the Holy Spirit in His multi-dimensional capacity. The Holy Spirit will influence the church so greatly individuals in the church will be divinity in action. Sometime ago, we were my church (not The Elevation Church's) was holding a seven-day crusade in Ijebu water side. On the last day of the crusade, as we began to minister the baptism of the Holy Spirit to the people there, I noticed that the person I was working with was struggling to get these people baptized, yet none was receiving the baptism of the Holy Ghost. I just left him with the understanding that ministering baptism of the Holy Spirit should be easier than that. Getting to a man, I could barely reach for his man's forehead when this man exploded in tongues.

Listen: what I am sharing with you is the platform for a revolutionary Christian adventure. There is going to be an invasion of divine verge in the last days But we will have to undertake an exciting adventure in the school of revival to ensure that the invasion does not end in our indignation.

Revelation is the gateway to revolution. It takes a pregnancy of revelation to give birth to revolution. After the destiny of Gideon was revealed to him, he went after the Midianites, and overthrew them. Every revolution is revelation-motivated.

Revolution is what I consider as received revelation in manifestation. Michael Faraday, one of the great inventors in the world history, had no formal education. He was a bookbinder in a press but had an insatiable thirst for knowledge. He would normally attend scientific lectures, and after listening to Sir Humphrey Davys' lecture, he gathered his notes, bound them and sent them to Sir Humphrey Davys.

Sir Humphrey was so impressed by Michael's work, that when his laboratory attendant left, he rode on horseback to search for Michael to invite him to work for him. Michael took up the job as Sir Humphrey's laboratory attendant and from there rose to become a giant in the field of science. In fact, he rose to become the envy of even Sir Humphrey, his former boss. Faraday later invented the electromagnetic generator, and also established electromagnetic in 1791, a discipline which is still relevant to our generation today

There is the Spirit of revelation. That is what Apostle Paul told us in Ephesians 1:17-18:

> *That the God of our Lord Jesus Christ, the Father of glory may give to you the spirit of wisdom and revelation in the knowledge of Him, the eyes of your understanding being enlightened, that you may know what is the hope of His calling, what are the riches of the glory of his inheritance in the saints.*

The Spirit of revelation opens you up for a positive and effective drive, and it motivates you for a positive and productive action. The Spirit of revelation is the vital force behind every major event in the history of time. It is the backbone of every man who ever positively affected his generation.

And, of course, if our generation must partake in this God-sent revival that is about to breakout, then, we must believe God for an unprecedented outpouring of the Spirit of revelation as promised in Joel chapter two:

> And it shall come to pass afterward that I will pour out My Spirit on all flesh; your sons and your daughters shall prophesy, your old men shall dream dreams, your young men shall see visions. And upon the servants and the handmaids in those days I will pour my Spirit.
>
> JOEL 2:28

It is our baptism of the Spirit of revelation that will position us for this move of God. And when this is accomplished, the church will assume its rightful place—a place of super excellence, and dictate the affairs of the world.

> You are the way you are because that's the way you want to be. If you really wanted to be any different, you would be in the process of changing right now.
> FRED SMITH

20

BORN
TO WIN

> You were born to win, but to be a
> winner, you must plan to win,
> prepare to win, and expect to win.
> ZIG ZIGLAR

I want to begin this chapter by saying:

Y ou are born a winner, you cannot afford to die a
loser. Christianity without power is mere
religion. Nothing is more peculiar than power.

Yes! You are born a winner! You are a heavyweight
champion. You are an unbeatable and indisputable winner.
The enemy that will ever dare to stay in the ring with you,
not to talk of defeating you, has not been born! The enemy
should sight you from afar and just clear off. Why? Because
you are a winner!

*Behold all those who were incensed against you shall be
ashamed and disgrace; they shall be as nothing and those
who strive with you shall perish. You shall seek them and not*

find them– those who contended with you. Those who war against you shall be as nothing, as an one existeth thing.
ISAIAH 41:11-12

You are a winner, not a loser. So, recover your destiny

Perhaps, you have been living like a loser all these years, I like to announce to you that your victory is just around the corner. You are not a loser. Victory sometimes can be likened to a man in an overall jacket called travail, and you may be tempted to call yourself a loser if you find yourself wearing one. Travail is not a loss, it is a gain. It is a gain because travail is naturally followed by triumph. For this reason, you cannot be correctly referred to as a loser, you are a winner. So start living like a winner. See how the prophet Isaiah buttressed my point:

Before she travailed, she brought forth, before her pain came, she was delivered of a manchild. Who hath heard such a thing? Who hath seen such things? Shall the earth be made to bring forth in one day? Or shall a nation be born at once? for as soon as Zion travailed, she brought forth her children.
ISAIAH 66:7-8 (KJV)

God is saying to you:

"Push! It is your turn to deliver. Don't just ponder. Don't just pray. Don't just praise. Push!!! Push tirelessly!"

To push is to put pressure on the word of God to produce for you. You are not a loser. You are not the defeated. You are not a struggler. You are not a parasite. No! No! No!

Your status has been changed at new birth. So, you are a winner. You are an achiever. You are a distributor. See yourself like that. Behave like that. Then, it will not be long before you begin to see yourself going from success to success, from victory to victory and from glory to glory!

> Then God said, "Let Us make man in Our image, after our likeness; let them have dominion over the fish of the sea, and over the fowl of the air, and over the cattle, over all the earth and over every creeping thing that creeps on the earth." So God created man in His own image; in the image of God He created him; male and female created He them. Then God blessed them, and God said to them, "Be fruitful and multiply; fill the earth and subdue it; have dominion…"
>
> GENESIS 1:26-28

This is a fantastic revelation.

After I gave my life to Christ, at night while I slept, some demons would oppress me in my dreams. After I received this revelation, instead of letting these demons oppress me, I began to torment them in my dream. Today the devil hardly bothers me like he does some people.

> Shall the prey be taken from the mighty, or the captives of the righteous be delivered? But thus says the LORD: "Even the captives of the mighty shall be taken away, and the prey of the terrible be delivered; for I will contend with him who contends with you, and I will save your children. I will feed those who oppress you with their own flesh, and they shall be drunk with their own blood as with sweet wine.
>
> ISAIAH 49:24-26

Friend, you are a bonafide member of God's ever-winning family! You are a spiritual powerhouse! You are too loaded with power to be a loser. Demons should sight you and cry, "Have you come to destroy us before the time?"

The Defeated Christians

The defeated Christians are the category of Christians in the church that have settled for mediocrity. They have inferiority complex. The sad thing about this class of people is that, they do not only fear the devil, but also encourage other people to do the same. They are like Job who at a point in his life called the devil the mighty one.

The Lukewarm Christians

The lukewarm Christians are the category of Christians in the church that have settled for mediocrity. They have inferiority complex. The sad thing about this class of people is that although they do not fear the devil, they do not have trust in God.

> I know your works, that you are neither cold nor hot. I could wish you were cold or hot. So then, because you are lukewarm, and neither cold nor hot, I will vomit you out of My mouth. Because you say, 'I am rich, have become wealthy, and have need of nothing'— and do not know that you are wretched, miserable, poor, blind, and naked— I counsel you to buy from Me gold refined in the fire, that you may be rich; and white garments, that you may be clothed, that the shame of your nakedness may not be revealed; and anoint your eyes

with eye salve that you may see. As many as I love, I rebuke and chasten. Therefore be zealous and repent.
REVELATION 3:15-19

The Victorious Christians

This is the category of Christians who may be described as the militant Christians. They believe Christianity is all about fighting battles. So they keep fighting and fighting the devil.

For whatever is born of God overcomes the world. And this is the victory that has overcome the world—our faith.
1 JOHN 5:4

The victorious Christians can also be said to be travailing Christians, and currently in the sheep stage in our Christian adventure.

Lastly we have…

The Triumphant Christians

Humorously, permit to say that this is the last but also the latest brand of Christians. It is the most advanced because it is the stage of life or sphere of existence that God originally intended for all mankind. It is the kind of life showcased in the Garden of Eden.

The triumphant Christians are the category of Christians who believe in the finished work of Jesus Christ. They believe Jesus had already fought and won Satan. So they do not start fighting an enemy that has totally been defeated by Jesus.

The triumphant Christians have the virtue, verdict and validity of their unarguable, true and lasting triumphant victory over the devil and his agents. They are the unbeatable world heavyweight winners, anyday anytime, and anywhere!

The triumphant Christians are the class of people that have come to grip with the fact that they are BORN TO WIN anyday anytime, anywhere!

Now thanks be to God who always leads us in triumph in Christ, and through us diffuses the fragrance of His knowledge by us in every place.

2 CORINTHIANS 2:14

Great things are not something accidental, but must certainly be willed.
VINCENT VAN GOGH, Artist

21

FAITH CAN CHANGE YOUR WORLD

> By faith we excel.
> AYO LAWAL

"Free at last…free at last…thank God Almighty, I'm free at last!" These powerful words of Martin Luther King Jr., stunned the world as he spoke them to the millions of people that watched on TV or listened over the radio in the 1960s. This divine movement, divine awakening and spirit-inspired message of Martin Luther King Jr., was conceived in a womb of the desire for a life of faith.

In Genesis 1:2-3, the Bible declares:

> *The earth was without form, and void; and darkness was on the face of the deep. And the Spirit of God was hovering over the face of the waters. Then God said, "Let there be light"; and there was light.*

His whole life was a battle on how to bring faith – Bible faith – back into the Church.

By faith we understand that the worlds were framed by the Word of God.

HEBREWS 11:3

Faith is creative, and is the force behind creation. All that we see today – the heavens and the earth, the animal kingdom, the plant kingdom, and the likes – were all brought into existence through the instrumentality of faith.

In Genesis 1:2-3, the Bible declares:

The earth was without form, and void; and darkness was on the face of the deep. And the Spirit of God was hovering over the face of the waters. Then God said, "Let there be light"; and there was light.

This is what faith is all about, exploring possibilities when impossibilities are staring you right in the face. God saw that the world around Him was ugly. And He brought out His faith tool, and began to prune the world until beauty came out of ugliness. And how did God get the job done? God began by speaking His desire into existence. God kept speaking and speaking and speaking until His word began to find practical expression in the world around Him. At that time, God set into motion what could be tagged the strategy of faith over failure.

Every man's way is interjected with challenges. There is no

insurmountable challenge. Every challenge can be overcome by faith. A challenge that looks insurmountable is evidence of the absence of faith.

Christianity without faith will be reduced to a frustrated religion. Faith is the livewire of Christianity; it is the anchor of Christianity. That is the reason why someone who has given his life to Christ will be said to be in the "faith." The totality of the Christian adventure is summarized as *the faith.*

Faith is not a Pentecostal emblem. It is operating in the realm of God. It is manifesting divinity. It is proclaiming what you believe and working at it until what you proclaim begins to manifest. In fact, take faith out of Christianity and you will be left with nothing. Absolutely nothing!

We are saved by faith. "For by grace you have been saved through faith, and that not of yourselves; it is the gift of God" (Ephesians 2:8).

We stand by faith. "Not that we have dominion over your faith, but are fellow worker for your joy; for by faith you stand" (2 Corinthians 1:24).

We walk by faith. "For we walk by faith, not by sight" (2 Corinthians 5:7).

We overcome by faith. "For whatever is born of God overcomes the world. And this is the victory that has overcome the world – our faith" (1 John 5:4).

We are kept by faith. "Who are kept by the power of God through faith for salvation ready to be revealed in the last time" (1 Peter 1:5).

We live by faith. "Now the just shall live by faith" (Hebrew 10:38).

We are healed by faith (Matthew 29:7-27).

Our "faith" is preserved by faith. "Having faith and a good conscience which some having rejected, concerning the faith have suffered shipwreck." (1 Timothy 1:19)

And, of course, faith has only one source– the word of God. "…Faith comes by hearing, and hearing by the word of God" (Romans 10:17).

It is the word of God that breeds faith. Just as river Nile has its source in Egypt, faith has its source in the word of God.

The heart is the factory of faith. "FOR WITH THE HEART ONE BELIEVES UNTO RIGHTEOUSNESS and with the mouth confession is made unto salvation" (Romans 10:10). That is the place where we were born, nurtured and grown.

You may ask, "How do I operate in faith?" You may ask again, "How do I turn my faith loose to do the impossible?"

First, you operate in faith by speaking it. "For with the heart man believes to righteousness and WITH THE MOUTH CONFESSION IS MADE TO SALVATION" (Romans 10:10).

If God, the Creator had to speak what He believe into existence why can't you?

Secondly you operate your faith by acting it. Or, by doing it. "For as the body without the spirit is dead, so faith without works is dead."(James 2:26)

Listen to this, it will help you. There is the Spirit of faith. The Spirit of faith is another dimension of the manifestation of the Holy Spirit. It is one of the pillars of Pentecostalism that the end-time church must embrace if we must move to the next level of our faith in God. You cannot be endowed with the Spirit of faith and not engage your mouth in laudable, positive and productive confessions.

> And since we have the same spirit of faith, according to what is written, "I believe and therefore I spoke," we also believe and therefore speak.
>
> 2 CORINTHIANS 4:13

So, friend, 'I am in the faith' is not a church emblem, it is accessing the realm of the possibilities. The Spirit of faith is an asset that guarantees our access into the realm of possibilities. It makes you unbeatable and irresistible.

Fear has torment.

Faith has pleasure.

Your fear is your fury.

Your faith is your future.

Fear is a killer. First, it will torment you. Then it will tear you. Then it will kill you. But thank God; there is an escape route for us today! We are not fortunate. We are "faithtunate."

In the late 90s, the wife of the resident pastor of the church where I worshipped at the time told me in a service that she would like to see me. Later, she came and showed me some gold jewelleries that she had been trying to sell but could not sell and asked me to agree with her in prayer I joined my hands with her in prayer of agreement in faith that those things be sold and that was it. She did not have to worry about selling the articles again after the prayer was said.

> Do the thing you fear and the
> death of fear is certain.
> EMERSON

22

WISDOM
FOR WINNING

> Wisdom is a defense;
> lack of it is an offense
> AYO LAWAL

We were never created for a defensive lifestyle. No! No! No! We were created to live an offensive Christian life. As it is said, offense is the best defence. If we must do the impossible, the camp of the enemy has to be invaded. Instead of waiting to ward off the devil – the discouragers, the critics, the opposition – and their onslaughts, we must turn the battle around and launch an invasion of an onslaught against the enemy's camp. This is the strategy of wisdom over wickedness. Friend, wisdom is a defense, lack of it is an offense. So let's go get it!

In Proverbs 3:19, the Bible says:

The Lord by wisdom founded the earth; by understanding he established the heavens.

Hear this too:

> *O LORD, how manifold are Your works! In wisdom You have made them all. The earth is full of You possessions.*
>
> PSALMS 104:24

This is fantastic. Friend, wisdom is a foundation. And, "if the foundations are destroyed, what can the righteous do?" (Psalm 11:3). That is to say no matter how righteous you are, if wisdom is not in place, you cannot do anything! Come on, let put wisdom in place and be on the offensive.

Wisdom is a kingdom fundamental factor for establishing dominion. Christianity without wisdom will be reduced to child's play. When God created the universe, it was on the platform of wisdom. When the devil started his trouble in heaven also, it was by wisdom that he was fired out of heaven.

> *And they overcame him by the blood of the Lamb, and by THE WORD OF THEIR TESTIMONY, and they did not love their lives to the death.*
>
> REVELATION 12:11 (Emphasis Mine)

Jesus kingdom strategy for defence is offense. He came to this world as a man of war to destroy the works of the devil. In fact, Christ took the battle to the enemies camp, invaded hell, and prevailed by completely defeating the devil and his cohorts. And wisdom was His weapon.

Wisdom is a weapon given by God to His holy Apostles and Prophets to reach their generation for Jesus. This passage that we have just read helps us to appreciate that wisdom has its ultimate source in the word of God. John said they overcame by the word of their testimony.

Also the writer of Hebrews tells us that the entire universe was created or brought into existence through the word of God. Let us see how he puts it:

> By faith we understand that the worlds were framed by THE WORD OF GOD.
>
> HEBREWS 11:3 (Emphasis Mine)

And John 1:1-3 says:

> In the beginning was the Word, and the Word was with God, and the Word was God. He was in the beginning with God. All things were made by Him, and without Him nothing was made that was made.

And 1 Corinthians 1:24 also says:

> But to those who are called, both Jew and Greeks, Christ the power of God and the wisdom of God.

All these go to show that the word through which the heavens and the earth, the animal kingdom, the plant kingdom, and all that we see today came into existence by the wisdom of God. In other words, the wisdom of God has its root in the word of God. It is this same word that Michael and his angels used to knock out the devil from heaven as earlier mentioned in Revelation 12:11.

The law of the LORD is perfect, converting the soul; the testimony of the LORD is sure, making wise the simple.
PSALM 19:7

So you can locate the word of God to contact the wisdom of God. When Solomon contacted this wisdom, no devil from the pit of hell could break into his territory. And the wisdom of God upon the life of Solomon became his asset; his access into the trouble-free zone of life.

This is how it works: the word of God makes you wise, and when you are wise, you cannot but emerge a winner. Show me a man of wisdom and I will show you a winner. Stop anointing the clothes of your spouse; your husband is not the problem; you need to go and get wisdom. And once this wisdom is lavished on you, you will not have to stain your spouse's clothes before you have a successful family life!

The whole land of Egypt would have been starved to death if not for the wisdom of God in the life of Joseph. Joseph offered Pharaoh a wisdom solution to a national problem. Pharaoh accepted the offer and the nation as a whole was preserved. Wisdom is the fastest track to doing the impossible. Joseph knew this.

Wisdom is the principal thing. Let us go and get it.

Wisdom is real. Wisdom is the birthright of everyone that is born of God. Bishop David Oyedepo has enjoyed a hitch-free family life for about three decades now, all on the application of the many-sided wisdom of God in its innumerable aspects and infinite varieties. If you are born again, the wisdom of God becomes your heritage. Wisdom, among other things, is one of our covenant redemptive package in God. And wisdom has its source in God's word.

> *And that from childhood you have known the Holy Scriptures, which are able to make you wise for salvation through faith which is in Christ Jesus.*
>
> 2 TIMOTHY 3:15

Matthew 7:24-26 tells us:

> *Therefore whoever hears these sayings of Mine, and does them, I will liken him to a wise man...but everyone that hears these sayings of Mine, and does not do them, we be like a foolish man...*

So you see, it is the practice of the word of God that makes a man wise. Until you learn to practice and do the word of God, you will never receive His wisdom.

Friend, wisdom can change your world. It can bring you out of obscurity into the limelight. It is the principal weapon in the days of battle. Let's go get it!

Faith moves mountains
Wisdom breaks mountains.
AYO LAWAL

23

LOVE CAN CHANGE
YOUR WORLD

If you could only love enough, you could be the
most powerful person in the world.
EMMET FOX

When we despise God's commandment, we will be damned by it. When we embrace God's commandment we will be lifted by it. Every step of obedience is a step into supernatural victory.

He who despises the word will be destroyed, but he that fears the commandment will be rewarded.

PROVERBS 13:13

You will not be destroyed, in Jesus name! Obedience is going to be our escape route from all oppression of the devil in these last days. Do you want your oppression to end? Then, start allying and complying with scriptural demands.

Love can change our world. Love is the all-important and

life-controlling commandment. See how the King of kings puts it:

> *This is My commandment, that you love one another as I have loved you.*
>
> JOHN 15:12

Do you get it now? Fine! We are in a lovers' world. To be loveless is to be lifeless. The old covenant had Ten Commandments. The new covenant has one, only one commandment–love.

The Bible tells us in 1 Corinthians 10:12 thus: "…love covers all sins." Love is the law of life. And all the law is fulfilled in it.

Do not get me wrong. I am not saying you have to disobey God by breaking the Ten Commandments. What I am saying is if you are walking in love, you will not have to bother yourself about the Ten Commandments. This is because the entire Ten Commandments are fulfilled in love.

Do you think God loves those "thou shall not…thou shall not" laws? I believe He does not. I believe God hates them, but had to establish them after Adam sinned.

God kept a tree, and Adam went and stole from its fruits. It was illegal. So God imposed laws. God knew that the descendants of Adam would not keep their hands off the 'fruits' on the tree. Even today, born-again, spirit-filled Christians break the Ten Commandments. But, praise

God! The end-time saints have finally found a way of escape, that is, love. I believe this is why one of the fruits of the Spirit is love (Galatians 5:23).

Life involves the collection of laws and principles. Applying these laws and principles can change your life...instantly...forever! And, of course, love is a major law in the school of life. It is the golden bridge to the greatest season we have longed for all our lives.

Reinhard Bonnke once wrote, "On the lips of Jesus the law becomes love." Friend, I can't agree more! Oh, what a friend we have in Jesus!

Love never fails..." (1 Corinthians 13:8).

Love never fears and Fear never loves.

Love is loaded in heaven. It is breeded by God as a spiritual fruit to all saints. Saints are full of love themselves like mango trees are full of mango fruits.

Fear on the other hand, is forged in hell, and it is issued by satan as a weapon to all demons. Demons are full of fear themselves, like scorpions are full of poison. They know its meaning. They know it has a paralyzing force. The devil wants to sting us all, making us sick with fear till we are paralysed by his counterfeit weapon. But they are illusions – fears are mere phantoms. They only take on substance if we accept them. We must reject fear. Fear is satan's venom. Love is God's antidote for fear. (1 John 4:18)

Wherever hatred reigns, failure reigns. Men continue to live in bondage. But wherever love reigns, success reigns. Men abound with blessings. Bishop David Oyedepo has been married for about thirty years now and is yet to have the first argument with his wife. Is that not wonderful? But it takes love to do it.

> *But as it is written, "Eyes has not seen, nor ear heard, nor have entered into the heart of man, the things which God has prepared for those who love Him."*
>
> 1 CORINTHIANS 2:9

Friend, it is your season of victory. This implies that all the showers we stand to enjoy in the kingdom are going to be on the platform of love. Solomon was the wealthiest man that ever lived on earth, but Solomon loved the Lord. If we want Solomon's blessings we must do it the way Solomon did it.

> *Jesus said to him, you shall love the LORD your God with all your heart, with all your soul, and with all your mind.*
>
> MATTHEW 22:37

So you see, it takes a heart for God to make a mark on earth. Love is of the heart. Without a genuine heart for God, there cannot be true victory in life. A genuine heart for God Is your golden door to the Eden you have searched for all your life.

Hatred breeds hindrances. Love breeds life. Fear kills success. Faith kills failure.

One of the key profits of love is success. Do you want success? Are you tired of business failure? Do you desire a hitch-free marital experience? Then, go for love. It is the cheapest way to be fulfilled.

Love is life. And Satan knows it. For example, David, because of his affection for God, single-handedly gave gold worth five hundred and seventy six million pounds ($576,000,000) for the building of the house of God. In fact, David didn't just give the gold, he also made sure that a place was found for the building of the house. No wonder, his affection commanded so much unction that he never lost a single battle.

The devil cannot stand a man that is greatly in love with God. Jesus said, "The thief does not come except to steal, and to kill, and to destroy. I am come that they may life, and that they may have it more abundantly" (John 10:10).

It was the same love for God that moved Daniel to open his windows and pray openly to God, under emphasizing the lion's den threat and over emphasizing his heart-felt love. And because Daniel was sold out to God, God saw to it that he succeeded in spite of the King's threat. Love lifted him.

The devil is a specialist love-destroyer. Beware of him! To be forewarned is to be forearmed. This testimony of Reverened Kenneth E. Hagin affirms what the premise of this chapter is all about:

I was healed more than fifty-five years ago in Mckinney, Texas as a Baptist boy reading grandma's Methodist Bible.

I was raised up from a deathbed, healed of two serious organic problems. My body was nearly totally paralysed because of a deformed heart, and I had an incurable blood disease. In fact, Dr. Robason, the fifth doctor on my case, said, 'Son, I'll be honest with you. If you didn't have the deformed heart and the paralysis, this incurable blood disease alone would prove to be fatal to you.' In all these years since I received my healing I continue to study the word of God along the lines of faith and healing. And, of course, you can't study faith and healing without studying love because the Bible says faith works by love. I have always made it my practice never to permit the least bit of animosity or ill-will in my heart against anyone. I can go five to seven years at a time and, from the standpoint of experiencing any discomfort, don't even know that I have a body. The only time I've ever been attacked with sickness is when I acted foolishly and didn't take care of my body, and when I didn't walk in love.

God is love. And God is everlasting. That means love is everlasting-eternal.

Owe no man anything except to love one another, for he who loves another has fulfilled the law. ROMANS 13:8

Love is an everlasting debt. First, towards God, and secondly to your fellow man. It is a debt you never get to pay. Some years ago, growing ministry needed to erect a church building and Bishop Oyedepo was privilege to be involved in drawing and designing it. Later, the pastor asked how much he wanted to be paid for his input; and tears began to stream down his cheeks. Bishop Oyedepo said all he kept thinking was: "Lord, if You give me money, I will build the church for them."

Friend, it is time we explore love's way. Love's way is the best way any day, anytime, anywhere! (1 Corinthians 12:31)

I am no longer a young man filled with energy and vitality. I'm given to meditation and prayer. I would enjoy sitting in a rocker, swallowing prescriptions, listening to soft music, and contemplating the things of the universe. But such activity offers no challenge and makes no contribution. I wish to be up and doing. I wish to face each day with resolution and purpose. I wish to use every waking hour to give encouragement, to bless those whose burdens are heavy, to build faith and strength of testimony. It is the presence of wonderful people which stimulates the adrenaline. It is the look of love in their eyes which gives me energy.

GORDON. B. HINCKLEY, age ninety-two

24

SATAN,
GET LOST!

> The ability to simplify means to eliminate the unnecessary so that the necessary may speak.
> HANS HOFMANN

Say to God, "How awesome are Your works! Through the greatness of Your power Your enemies shall submit themselves to You."

PSALM 66: 3

Have you ever pondered this incredible truth in your heart: the most excellent is also the most powerful! The psalmist declares God as the highest power. So God is the most excellent because He is most powerful. You know we call Him Omni-potent God which means to say the all powerful God.

Thus from this scriptural perspective, I believe power is a major prerequisite for excellence.

Therefore I trust God, the all powerful God, to charge you

with so much power that all the challenges of your life will be easily chased away. Presently you may be faced with a Goliath-challenge staring at you in the face, roaring at you like a lion and you don't know what you need to change your situation.

Don't turn away. You belong to the Lion family. The strongest among all that does not turn away for any.

What you need is power. And what you have is power. The power you will ever need to produce the change you desire most is available to you today. "Today I give you power", says the Lord.

What is power? Power is the ability to effect change. Even Moses in the prototype that God gave us in the exodus of the Israelites could not do what was impossible for 430 years until power came on to the scene. That is why God told the Israelite to remember He was the One that gave them the power to do the impossible (Deuteronomy 8:18). Do you want to do the impossible? Do you really, really want to do the impossible? Then, you need to encounter God's power.

Power. A very important word for this generation. As an individual, a community or a nation that is in pursuit of possibilities, I believe power should be our watchword. For until our thirst for power is in place, our desire for the achievement of possibilities is fake.

Until we learn to develop an insatiable appetite for the power of God, our dream of excellence is far from being achieved. That won't be your portion, in Jesus name! So let's stop celebrating our weakness, and let's start commanding power.

David commanded power and many days harassment that the Israelites army had suffered was terminated in a single day. So when next a Goliath knocks at your door, make sure God is at home with you.

The end-time church is a church of power. It is a reigning church. It is a shining church, but the church is going to shine on the platform of power. And as the saints in the church are shining, the enemy will be suffering. Life will be so unbearable for the devil that he would say "Oh God, let Your kingdom come!" That the excellency of power may be of God.

Way back in 1979, Bishop Oyedepo was preaching somewhere and after preaching he said "If you know that you are a witch, stand on your feet." Some people responded. Then he called one of the people standing and asked, "How do you operate?" The witch replied, "We go to the highway and when we see a vehicle coming, we cause an accident and suck blood of the victims." Without hesitating, the Bishop asked again, "What do you do when people like me are coming?" The witch replied, "When we sense a higher power, we clear off the highway"

This is what I am talking about…

Please get ready saint of God because there is about to be an unusual outburst of power around you.

The first man, Adam was a man enthroned with such power. Every wild beast was submissive to his authority, and even satan, the old serpent, could not question his authority.

However, once Adam sinned, he lost his authority! And he was banished from Eden, the power zone. Thus, Adam became a servant where he was once a ruler. But, praise God! It did not end there.

That is what Paul told us in Ephesians 2:4-6:

> But God, who is rich in mercy, because of His great love with which he loved us, even when we were dead in trespasses, made us alive together with Christ (by grace you have been saved), and raised us up together, and made us sit together in the heavenly places in Christ Jesus.

In other words, Jesus died and rose in order to restore man to his original position of power.

> And war broke out in heaven. Michael and his angels fought with the dragon, and the dragon and his angels fought, But they did not prevail, nor was a place found for them in heaven any longer. So the great dragon was cast out, that serpent of old, called the devil and satan, who deceives the whole world; he was cast to the earth, and his angels were cast out with him. Then I heard a loud voice saying in heaven, "Now is come salvation, and strength, and the kingdom of our God, and the power of His Christ have come. For the accuser of our

brethren, who accused them before our God day and night, has been cast down"

REVELATION 12:7-10

So, from scriptural perspective, we are now in heaven where there is no place for the devil. So we are now in heaven where the power of Christ is our right. Our status has been changed at new birth. We now reside in a brand-new world; a world without limit or boundary; a place the enemy has no say; and a realm you and I can tap into the power of the world to come.

Friend, the trumpet is already blowing, announcing your departure from the elementary class in the school of power to a higher class. We have had enough "mouthfestation" of the power of God. It is time for the manifestation of the power of God.

Alleluia!

The eyes of your understanding being enlightened, that you may know what is the hope of his calling, what are the riches of the glory of His inheritance in the saints, And what is the exceeding greatness of His power to us who believe, according to the working of His mighty power, Which He worked in Christ when He raised Him from the dead, and seated Him at His right hand in the heavenly places, Far above all principality and power and dominion, and every name that is named, not only in this age but also in that which is to come. And He put all things under His feet, and gave Him to be the head over all things to the church.

EPHESIANS 1:18-22

The African man may never stop being a sufferer, because according to him, the devil is always the reason for his calamity. What a great mistake! We are not born again to suffer again. New birth confer on us absolute dominion over satan and his cohorts; satan is a defeated foe.

For us to still see him as the source of our suffering is an abuse on our redemption. We are not in his class, we are superior to him. The scripture tells us that we are far, far above him. It is high time we take our rightful place in God. Until we do this, doing the impossible is an elusive dream. So brace up and get set. Power is about to explode!

We do not have to start fighting a battle that has already been fought and won by Jesus. Jesus has completely defeated satan, the enemy. Salvation is what terminates slavery. Redemption is the cure for oppression. For you to still be living under the fear of Satan is a slap on redemption!

> *For sin shall not have dominion over you, for you are not under law but under grace.*
>
> ROMANS 6:14

Sin and satan are synonymous. What the Bible says here applies to Satan also because sin and Satan weigh the same. Sin and satan were crushed at cavalry about two thousand years ago. So you can always organize yourself out of their circle. You can always calculate that negative situation out of your life. It is all up to you. Make your choice—now!

The first time I found myself in the midst of armed robbers

was 1995. I did not cringe like a scared cat or a cringing coward because I knew better. All eyes were heavily soaked in tears except mine. Why? I possessed a superiority mentality. The witch living next door to you is not your problem. Your ignorance is your greatest undoing. Bishop Oyedepo said, "There is no mountain anywhere, every man's ignorance is his own mountain."

Of course, it is true. Every affliction that a man suffers is either because of satan, sin or ignorance. And now that you have located the source of your trouble, all you need to do is to technically loosen yourself from the grip of satan, sin or ignorance. The hour has finally come for you to level your mountain and fill up your valley. So brace up!

Let's study a little of history here. According to history, before the development of human civilization, power was a function of physiology. Then, the physically strong and fast were the most powerful. As human civilization developed, power resulted from heritage. For instance, if you were a king, chief or the likes then you would be said to have power. If you permit me, we can call that "title" power. We see this heresy all around us today. We see different leaders – spiritual, political, community, etc – all around the world with big, big titles as it were without any form of power to back them up. Why? The era of physical or title power is gone.

Then, came the days of the industrial age when capital represented power. But that era too is gone. Mind you, all these things still play a major role in our achievement in life. It is better to have them than not to. But they are not the ultimate source of the force that liberates us.

However, recently the largest source of power has been knowledge– specialized knowledge, if you permit me to say I remember back then in my primary school, we had this small piece of cloth attached to the chest pocket of our school shirt. They call it our school badge then. On this piece of clothing material, you will find the logo of the school and the motto which reads: knowledge is power. Unfortunate I can tell that some of the students that passed out from that school ended up powerless, helpless and may be also useless Why? Knowledge ordinarily is not power. Oh, no! It is the correct application of knowledge that is power.

Like a notable author puts it, if there is anything that characterizes this modern world, it is the massive almost unimaginable, flow of information. I believe the correct utilization of this blizzard of data help us to exercise our dominion over sin and satan As John K. Galbraith writes:

Money fuelled the industrial society. But in the information society the fuel, the power, is knowledge. One has now come to see a new class structure divided by those who have information and those who must function out of ignorance. This new class has its power not from money, not from land, but from knowledge

Today wisdom has been said to be the proven source of power....so knowledge is not power; it is wisdom – the correct application of knowledge– that is power. Let me share a story of how Dr. Lester Sumrall used his knowledge of his authority over the devil to humiliate satan some years ago.

Dr. Sumrall found himself in a particular jungle in Africa. There he found a witch doctor reciting some incantations, making some concoction and pouring this concoction into the mouth of a frog and then drinking from the concoction from the mouth of the frog.

After watching this witch doctor for some time, Dr. Sumrall ministered to this witch doctor. Then and there, the witch doctor fell under the power of God, got saved and received the baptism of the Holy Spirit on the same day

Later that day when Dr. Sumrall got home, he discovered that there was a noise in his room. He went to see what was happening and saw that the curtains were shaking violently against the walls, the bed was moving violently back and forth. Then Dr. Sumrall cried out, "Devil! Get out of here." The noise stopped, the curtain stopped shaking back and forth and the bed also stopped moving back and forth. Then Dr. Sumrall cried out, "Devil! Get out of here." The noise stopped, the curtain stopped shaking back and forth and the bed also stopped moving back and forth. Then, Dr. Sumrall cried out once again, "Devil! Come back here! When I came in the curtains were standing quietly against the wall. The bed was standing beside the wall. So put them back in the name of Jesus!" spontaneously and momentarily, the noise started again. The curtain shook violently back to their position against the walls. The bed moved violently back to its position beside the wall. This is what power can do.

Power puts people in commad. Friend, it is your turn to gain command. Bishop David Oyedepo also shared a unique perspective on how he demonstrated his understanding of his power over satan many years back:

Sometime sago, while meditating on John 1, I saw how cheaply one can destroy the stronghold of darkness with light. I discovered that there is no contesting the supremacy of light in any conflict against darkness. I discovered the power of light.

Shortly after I went to my home town for Christmas and was told that one of my cousins had been afflicted with insanity. When I learnt this, I was excited, because I saw an opportunity to manifest the truth of the Word I had just encountered.

So I went to the room where he was. And as soon as I entered, he prostrated to greet me, he could recognize me in his mad state! I asked his brothers to put him in my car, saying, 'Let me see the devil that will follow him into my car.' We had scarcely driven a few kilometers when this cousin of mine fell sound asleep (he had not slept in days)!

When he was taker to the teaching hospital the following day he was asked, 'What is wrong with you?' But he replied, 'Do you mean what was wrong with me or what is wrong with me?' The doctors needed no further proof that he was healed! The same young man has since graduated from the university and is now working.

Friend, you are not born again to suffer again. How? The

key to power today is available to us all. The devil has blinded our minds for too long. It is time we loosen ourselves from every grip of Satan. It is time we begin to access the gems in the information that are exploding all around us today and using them to engage our mind in a logical, rational, and analytical thinking. It is time we adopt the prodigal son system of breakthrough…thinking through to effect change in the right direction in our quest to do the impossible. We can all unleash the power to do the rational, and analytical thinking. It is time we adopt the prodigal son system of breakthrough…thinking through to effect change in the right direction in our quest to do the impossible. We can all unleash the power to do the impossible within us. All we simply need to do is to learn how to engage our mind in the most powerful and productive and advantageous way like the prodigal son did in the bible story

Remember: You have the mind of Christ, not the mind of crisis. So go recover your destiny

Please say out loudly: "satan! Get lost."

So the next time you hear the devil roaring like a lion, what do you do? You spit on his face, defy him and tell him to get lost.

A man who suffers before it is necessary
suffers more than is necessary.
SENECA

25

FORGET NOT!

> You can't hold a man down
> without staying down with him.
> BOOKER T WASHINGTON

From the rising of the sun to its going down the LORD's name is to be praised.

PSALMS 113:3

Friend, the era power is here. We are in the era of power; the era where the blind see, the lame walk, the lepers are cleansed, the deaf hear, the dead are raised, the poor have the gospel preached to them at a natural frequency; the age where God's people are doing the impossible to the glory of God.

And of course, this era of power must also be the era of praise. Or, we will be drain with the power until it is reduced to pain. So it is the praiseful that will be powerful. No praise, no power!

We are in the season of the supernatural. The season where man must raise his hands in praise to God on earth if God must release His power from heaven. It is the praiseful that will survive this season. Why? God says, "Whoever offers praise glorifies Me." (Psalms 50:23).

What we do in praise is giving God the glory. To refuse to give the glory is to end up being grounded, because God will not give His glory to another. Neither will He share His praise with another. And if anyone tries to hijack God's glory, God will see to it that such a person does not live to tell the story. Micah, Saul's daughter, despised David's praise of God and became the only woman who died barren throughout the history of the Bible. That will never be your own portion in Jesus' name! God delights in our praise. Let us give it to Him.

Like a song writer wrote, shout hallelujah anyhow! Whether you do it in English, French or Spanish is irrelevant; shout hallelujah to the glory of God. You may even do it in your local dialect. And when you do, the song writer said, do it anyhow. That was exactly what David did.

All the glory belongs to God. When we give what belongs to God to Him, God will give us what belongs to us. Like God lifted David, God will see to it that we are also lifted to an enviable height. Unlike Micah, God will see to it that we live to share the testimony.

What Is Praise?

Praise is a spiritual device designed by God to connect man

with God. What we do in praise is provoking divine supernatural presence of God. We compel the Omnipotent hand of the Almighty to intervene on our behalf

Bishop David said, "Praise is the atmosphere for the fearsome acts of God." And it's true. That is what Moses also told us in Exodus 15:11:

Who is like You, O LORD, among the gods? Who is like You, glorious in holiness, fearful in praises, doing wonders?

Praise is the gateway to the fearful acts of God. It is door to the realms of signs and wonders. Have you ever considered the man David in the Bible? David's life epitomized a life of continual praise. He was a praise whiz. No wonder, he enjoyed such level of unquestionable and unchallengeable peace. He dwelled in the more-than-a-conqueror realm of life.

> Now it came to pass when the king was dwelling in his house, and the Lord had given him rest from all his enemies all round.
>
> 2 SAMUEL 7:1

This is what praise can do.

David encouraged us to cultivate this same lifestyle. He said:

> *Let everything that has breath praise the Lord. Praise the Lord!*
>
> PSALMS 150:6

Please don't forget this: We are debtors of God. Our life is a gift from God. Even after we are saved, our life is still a gift from God; it is by faith that we are saved. That is why we owe it to God to praise Him. Whether you have food, clothes, shelter or not, does not matter. Whether you are young or old is irrelevant. As long as you have breath, you are commanded to praise the Lord. Praise the Lord. Shout hallelujah anyhow!

Hallelujah!

Listen to this: Though you are paying a debt by fulfilling a commandment to praise God, the irony is that, your obedience to this commandment still positions you to tap into the benefits that praise carries. In this edition, I would like to share with you one out of the countless benefits of praise.

Divine Intervention

One of the benefits of praise, among other ones, is divine intervention. Every genuine praise naturally enjoys divine intervention in every area of life – spiritual, physical, ministry, business etc. Show me a man with a praise-filled life and I will behold a man with perpetual victory.

God will put His praise in our mouth in order to render our enemy helpless, useless and powerless. That is to say any time you are confronted with a situation that seems like a mountain before you, just arm yourself with the instrument of praise and the mountain will be cheaply dismantled. By the power of praise, every mountain before you will be levelled and every valley will be filled up.

An Old Testament king by the name Jehoshaphat and his people understood this pertinent secret. When they were confronted with battle, all they had to do was engage the weapon of praise. And guess what happened? They won!

> Now when they began to sing and to praise, the LORD set ambushes against the children of Ammon, Moab and Mount Seir, who had come against Judah; and they were defeated.
>
> 2 CHRONICLES 20:22

I stumbled on this testimony while writing this book. I think it will help you to grasp what I am talking about.

After I had my last baby six years ago, I have been believing God for the fruit of the womb. In June 1998, the Bishop declared a three-day captivity turning prayer and fasting meeting. During the programme, he said, 'The next six months is too much for God to make your laughter a reality.' I then said to God, 'If you give me a child I will give the testimony before the brethren.' At the Hosanna Night in July the Bishop asked us to write what we wanted on a paper and dance over it. By August, I became pregnant and this is the baby. We named him David. I give God all the glory.'
FUNSHO , J

I saw this one too and I believe it will also bring clarity to my point.

While traveling to the school where I applied for admission, I began reading the Bishop's book, Understanding the Power of Praise. On page eighteen, the Bishop says, 'God is about to do something in your life now. Are you ready to praise Him' I answered, 'Yes Papa', because it was like the bishop was talking to me face to face. Then I started praising God. When I got to the school, I could not find my name on the list, so I went to the man in charge of admission, who checked the list with him and said my name was there. He apologized for the error and included my name on the admission list. I give all the glory to God."

DANIELS, B

So you see, friend, just a moment of praise can terminate many years of pains. So develop a genuine heart of praise. Count your blessings. Cultivate a lifestyle of gratitude. That way, you will be unbeatable and unstoppable any day, anytime, anywhere!

The world of possibilities is a world of the saints of God. It is a world without satan; in the world of possibilities, the spirit of heaviness is being exchanged for the garment of praise, and the oil of joy is been traded for the ashes of mourning. It is the sphere of existence where nothing is impossible. Where there is no law, rules or boundary just limitless possibilities, and praise is the ticket there. Go get it!

And when you do, please don't forget to shout hallelujah!

Shout hallelujah, anyhow!

Feeling gratitude and not expressing it is like wrapping a present and not giving it.
WILLIAM ARTHUR WARD, Scholar

Doing The Impossible — 190

LION AND THE L AMB

Words & Lyrics By Crystal Lewis

Who is He who's the mightiest of all?
Who is He, creation trembles at His call?
Who is He, the lowly sacrifice,
Who paid a victim's price
His name is Jesus
Jesus from the Father's own right hand
Jesus Son of God and Son of Man
Jesus who died and rose again
Jesus He's the Lion and the Lamb

Who is He with the power none can tame?
Who is He that every foe would fear His name?
Who is He who was humbly led away
To suffer that dark day
His name is Jesus
Jesus from the Father's own right hand
Jesus Son of God and Son of Man

Jesus,who died and rose again
Jesus,He's the Lion and the Lamb

He's the Lion and the Lamb
He's the Lamb that was slain,
He's the Lion that reigns;
My Savior and King
Both the same

Who is He with the eyes that burn like fire?
Who is He? Oh, the wonder He inspires
Who is He who bore the guilt and shame

For those who'd gone astray
His name is Jesus
Jesus, from the Father's own right hand (oh yeah yeah)
Jesus, Son of God and Son of Man
Jesus, who died and rose again
Jesus, He's the Lion and-

He is Jesus, from the Father's own right hand
Jesus, Son of God and Son of Man
Jesus, who died and rose again
Jesus, He's the Lion and the Lamb
He's the Lion and the Lamb
He's the Lion and the Lamb

G E M ENTERPRISES®
EDUCATE. EMPOWER. ENTERTAIN.

FOR MORE INFORMATION
info@gementerpriseng.com

+234.816.181.6869

www.gementerprisesng.com

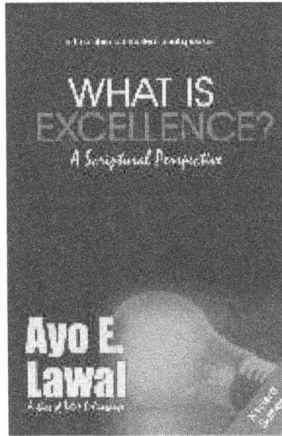

What is Excellence?
Ayo Lawal

Excellence is moving from struggle to survival, from survival to stability, from stability to success, from success to relevance, submitted Ayo. In this one-of-a-kind book, Ayo shares his foundational truths of excellence through personal anecdotes, biblical illusions and real-life examples from business, politics, sports, religion, and the military. He guides his readers through a series of questions, that, when answered, help individuals and teams achieve excellence. Undertake exciting adventure into a threshold of excellence that will change your life…instantly…forever!

Know someone who might be interested in a book by Ayo Lawal?
Why not share it with them – NOW!

ISBN: 978-978-931-9046 . Paperback . 180 pages

GEM ENTERPRISES

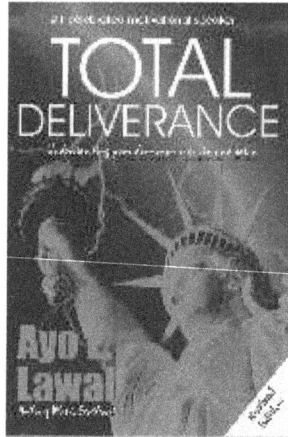

Total Deliverance
Ayo Lawal

Oh, yes! Total deliverance is the will of God for man. This truth is based on the prototype that God gave us in the exodus of a band of Hebrews from the oppressive rule of the Egyptian Pharaoh in the then-known Egypt, and the holistic profiles of men and women who enjoyed true freedom in their days. But why do many still live in captivity? Does it mean that deliverance is not possible today? Or, could it be that they must have mistaken deliverance for something else? In this power-packed book, Ayo presents us, vital keys to true and lasting deliverance. The insights shared in it will touch your life radically…forever!

Know someone who might be interested in a book by Ayo Lawal?
Why not share it with them – NOW!

ISBN: 978-978-931-9046 . Paperback . 180 pages

GEM ENTERPRISES

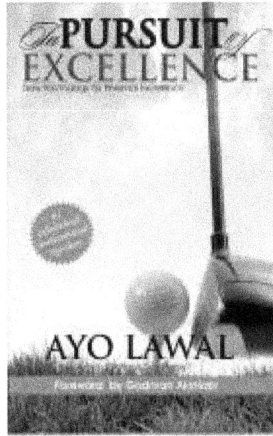

In Pursuit of Excellence
Ayo Lawal

Martin Luther King Jr. once said, "If a man hasn't discovered something that he will die for, he isn't fit to live." In this chart-blustering book, Ayo Lawal masterfully presents us with an insightful and empowering teaching on how to be our best…and even go beyond our best in our pursuit of excellence. "The greatest discovery in life is the discovery of self", he emphasized. "Self-discovery therefore is the beginning of excellence", he added. Wouldn't you like to be inspired by a God-inspired, power-packed and life-transforming book – to shorten your learning curve, beautify your experience and accelerate your achievement? Make it easy on yourself NOW. Get the five technologies for personal excellence. Get started with In Pursuit of Excellence-TOD AY!

Know someone who might be interested in a book by Ayo Lawal?
Why not share it with them – NOW!

ISBN: 978-978-931-9046 . Paperback . 189 pages

GEM ENTERPRISES

AYO LAWAL

is a renowned excellence expert, speaker, and author who has sold many copies of his life-transforming, destiny-moulding and joy-instigating books. Mr. Lawal founded GEM Enterprises and Ayo Lawal International, organisations that have been helping people excel all around the world. Every year he speaks to churches, companies, leaders, and organisations. Fast-selling author, Lawal's What is Excellence? and Total Deliverance have sold many copies. You can read his blog at AyoLawal.com, follow him at Twitter.com/AyoELawal, like him on Facebook at AyoELawal/facebook.com and learn more about him at AyoLawal.com

www.ingramcontent.com/pod-product-compliance
Lightning Source LLC
Chambersburg PA
CBHW051345200326
41521CB00014B/2484